BRADSHAW'S GUIDE TO BRUNEL'S RAILWAYS

Volume Three: The Minor Lines

John Christopher

AMBERLEY PUBLISHING

About this book

This book is intended to encourage the reader to explore many aspects of railway travel on Brunel's branch lines. Through Bradshaw's account and the supportive images and information it describes the history of the railways, their engineering works, architecture and some of the many changes that have occurred over the years. Hopefully it will encourage you to delve a little deeper when exploring Brunel's works, but please note that public access and photography is sometimes restricted for reasons of safety and security.

First published 2014

Amberley Publishing
The Hill, Stroud
Gloucestershire, GL5 4EP

www.amberley-books.com

Copyright © John Christopher, 2014

The right of John Christopher to be identified as the Author of this work has been asserted in accordance with the Copyrights, Designs and Patents Act 1988.

ISBN 978 1 4456 2178 4
EBOOK 978 1 4456 2193 7

British Library Cataloguing in Publication Data.
A catalogue record for this book is available from the British Library.

Typeset in 9.5pt on 12pt Celeste.
Typesetting by Amberley Publishing.
Printed in the UK.

Bradshaw on Brunel

This is the third volume in Amberley's series of books based on *Bradshaw's Descriptive Railway Hand-Book of Great Britain and Ireland* which was originally published in 1863. The first volume covered the journey on Brunel's mainline from Paddington all the way to Penzance in Cornwall – via the Great Western Railway, of course, but also the Bristol & Exeter, the South Devon Railway and the two Cornwall railways. Likewise in the second we took the train from Swindon Junction, headed up through the Sapperton Tunnel to Stroud and then up through Gloucester and across the River Severn to South Wales, all the way to Pembrokeshire. Brunel had been engineer on all of these railways and the two journeys covered a great many miles. However, the headlong rush from A to B, from terminus to terminus, did not offer the opportunity to explore the various offshoots or branch lines that spread outwards like tendrils of mostly broad gauge network. That is where this volume comes into its own as we take time to travel on the so-called 'Minor Lines'. But don't be put off by that term for we shall visit a fascinating selection of destinations from the City of Spires, great castles and even little Adlestrop – a stop remembered in poetry but otherwise little known. Along the way we shall encounter the last private battle on English soil and some remarkable survivors from Brunel's era.

A broad gauge train about to depart from Paddington, depicted by William Powell Frith, 1862.

Robert Howlett's iconic photograph of Isambard Kingdom Brunel standing in front of the chains at Millwall, on London's Isle of Dogs, during the construction of the steamship *Great Eastern*. This was the third and final of Brunel's three 'Great' ships.

George Bradshaw and Isambard Kingdom Brunel were close contemporaries who both enjoyed considerable success in their chosen fields and died while relatively young. Bradshaw, born in 1801, died in 1853 at the age of fifty-two, while Brunel, who was born just a few years later in 1806, was fifty-three years old when he died in 1859.

In all likelihood the two men never met, but their names were drawn together by an unprecedented transport revolution which took place during their brief lifetimes. It was Brunel and his fellow engineers who drove the railways, with their cuttings, embankments and tunnels, through a predominantly rural landscape to lay the foundations of the nineteenth-century industrial powerhouse that has shaped the way we live today. It is fair to say that the railways are the Victorians' greatest legacy to the twentieth and twenty-first centuries. They shrank space and time. Before their coming different parts of the country had existed in local time based on the position of the sun, with Bristol, for example, running ten minutes behind London. The Great Western Railway changed all that in 1840 when it applied synchronised railway time throughout its area. The presence of the railways defined the shape and development of many of our towns and cities, they altered the distribution of the population and forever changed the fundamental patterns of our lives. For many millions of Britons the daily business of where they live and work, and travel between the two, is defined by the network of iron rails laid down nearly two centuries ago by Brunel, his contemporaries, and an anonymous army of railway navvies.

The timing of the publication of Bradshaw's guidebooks is interesting. This particular account is taken from the 1863 edition of the handbook although, for practical reasons, it must have been written slightly earlier, probably between 1860 and 1862. By this stage the railways had lost their pioneering status, and with the heady days of the railway mania of the 1840s over they were settling into the daily business of transporting people and goods. By the early 1860s the GWR's mainline from London to Bristol, for example, had been in operation for around twenty years and was still largely in its original as-built form. It was also by this time that rail travel had become sufficiently commonplace to create a market for Bradshaw's guides.

As a young man George Bradshaw had been apprenticed to an engraver in Manchester in 1820, and after a spell in Belfast he returned to Manchester to set up his own business as an engraver and printer specialising principally in maps. In October 1839 he produced the world's first compilation of railway timetables. Entitled *Bradshaw's Railway Time Tables and Assistant to Railway Travelling,* the slender cloth-bound volume sold for sixpence. By 1840 the title had changed to *Bradshaw's Railway Companion* and the price doubled to one shilling. It then evolved into a monthly publication with the price reduced to the original and more affordable sixpence.

Although George Bradshaw died in 1853 the company continued to produce

'I say Holmes, is that really you?' Sherlock Holmes had cunningly disguised himself as a famous detective.

Above left: George Bradshaw was Brunel's close contemporary; the two men were born and died relatively young within a few years of each other. There is no record of the two men having met. *Above right*: Two distinguished, albeit fictional, travelers on Brunel's minor lines. In *The Boscombe Valley Mystery*, Sherlock Holmes and Dr Watson travelled by train through the 'beautiful Stroud valley', as Watson describes it, on their way to Ross-on-Wye.

Below: A broad gauge passenger express at full tilt near Uffington. The broad gauge could so easily have been Brunel's greatest engineering contribution, but it wasn't to be. *See page 22.*

THE FIRST "BRADSHAW"

A reminiscence of Whitsun Holidays in Ancient Egypt. From an old-time tabl(e)ature

Above: Punch's take on the ubiquitous guides and timetables. 'Seldom has the gigantic intellect of man been unemployed upon a work of greater utility.'

the monthly guides and in 1863 it launched Bradshaw's *Descriptive Railway Hand-Book of Great Britain and Ireland* (which forms the basis of this series of books). It was originally published in four sections as proper guidebooks without any of the timetable information of the monthly publications. Universally referred to as *Bradshaw's Guide* it was this guidebook that features in Michael Portillo's *Great British Railway Journeys*, and as a result of its exposure to a new audience the book found itself catapulted into the best-seller list almost 150 years after it was originally published.

Without a doubt the *Bradshaw Guides* were invaluable in their time and they provide the modern-day reader with a fascinating insight into the mid-Victorian rail traveller's experience. In 1865 *Punch* had praised Bradshaw's publications, stating that 'seldom has the gigantic intellect of man been employed upon a work of greater utility'. Having said that, the usual facsimile editions available nowadays don't make especially easy reading with their columns of close-set type. There are scarcely any illustrations for a start, and attempts to trace linear journeys from A to B are interrupted by distracting branch line diversions. That's where this volume comes into its own. *Bradshaw's Guide to Brunel's Railways, Volume 2,* takes the reader on a continuous journey from Swindon via Gloucester all the way to Pembrokeshire. The locations of Bradshaw's diversions on to the branch line routes are indicated in the text in square brackets, but for the most part these have been grouped in a final section in order to maintain the flow of our journey. The illustrations show scenes from Victorian times and they are juxtaposed with new photographs of the locations as they are today. The accompanying information provide greater background detail on Brunel, his railways and the many locations along the route.

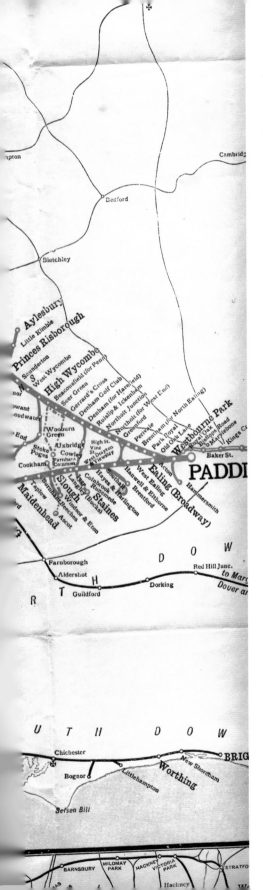

The railways

Although the railway map, published in the 1920s, shows the huge triangular territory of the GWR, various parts were originally built and operated by a number of independent companies. The lines described in this volume have been arranged in approximate order going from east to west from London. They include the Slough to Windsor branch and Didcot up to Oxford, which is followed by the Oxford, Worcester & Wolverhampton Railway – otherwise known less respectfully as the 'Old Worse & Worse' – and then the various Wilshire and Somerset branches including the line through Frome down to Salisbury. We also travel across from Gloucester on the South Wales Railway to the junction at Grange Court to take the Hereford, Ross & Gloucester line and, finally, explore the Taff Vale and Valley lines up to Abergavenny and Pontypool. As Bradshaw was concerned with the more direct routes some Brunellian lines, such as his Bristol & Gloucester Railway, are not covered as the guide covered the principal stopping points on other journeys, and in some cases the coverage of these arteries is somewhat patchy and the descriptive patches have assembled from other sections.

One final note: If you are wondering why Bradshaw makes no mention of the lines to Cardigan or Aberystwyth, for example, it is because these had not been completed by the time that the *Hand-Book* was published. The Aberystwyth & West Coast Railway, built as standard gauge, only opened to Aberystwyth in 1864, while the Carmarthen & Cardigan Railway, which was broad gauge initially, ran into financial difficulties and was not completed until much later, in 1895.

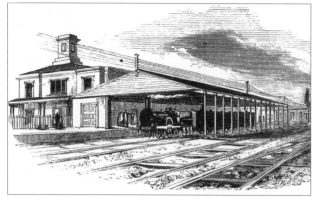

Left: Slough station was one of two built by Brunel as single-sided stations. The other was Reading. This layout featured Up and Down platforms beside each other but the requirement for trains to cross over the lines was a recipe for disaster and both stations were later rebuilt in the conventional manner.

Above: J. C. Bourne's etching of the newly opened Slough station focusses more on the station's exterior appearance.

Left: A more recent view of Slough station with a Class 165 waiting at the platform for the branch to Windsor *(Ibagli)*

Slough–Windsor Branch

SLOUGH

A telegraph station.

HOTEL – Crown.

MARKET DAY – Thursday.

After the bustle incident to the arrival of fresh passengers, and the departure of others, has in some degree subsided, it will be found that the arrangements for the comfort and convenience of those alighting at this station are equal, if not superior, to those of any other line.

A magnificent hotel, for aristocratic visitors, here so frequently found, is within a few minutes' walk, and numerous taverns, less ornamental, and, consequently, less expensive, are in the immediate neighbourhood.

Slough is now chiefly noticeable as the station or medium of communication, by the branch railway, to Eton and Windsor. It is two and a half miles in length, and passes Eton College, near the Thames.

WINDSOR

A telegraph station.

HOTELS – Castle; White Hart.

MARKET DAYS – Wednesday and Saturday.

FAIRS – Easter Tuesday, 5 July, 25 October.

This is a parliamentary borough (two members), with a population of 9,520 and a few public buildings, such as the Town Hall, built 1686, containing several royal portraits, and the modern church, in which are some of G. Gibbon's carvings; but the chief attractions are the *Castle* and Park, the seat of her majesty *the Queen*, and of her ancestors from the period of the Conquest.

WINDSOR is built on the banks of the Thames and has long been celebrated for its royal Castle and Park. It is situated on a hill which commands a delightful prospect over the adjacent country. It was first built by William the Conqueror, soon after his being seated on the throne of this kingdom. Edward III was born here, and had such an affection for the spot that he caused the old building to be pulled down, and a magnificent palace to be erected on its site, under the direction of the celebrated William of Wykeham; and re-established the princely order of the Garter.

No Briton can view unmoved the stately towers of 'Windsor's castled keep.' The mind is irresistibly carried back to the time when the Norman conqueror so far bent the stubborn necks of our Saxon ancestors, as to compel them to extinguish their fires on the sound of the innovating curfew. Rival houses have in turn held regal sway within its storied walls. Its history is the history of our

Left and below:
Two views of Windsor & Eton station as it is today. It opened in 1849 as Windsor station, and only after the college had been persuaded that its proximity would not lead the boys astray. Part of the station has been made into the Windsor Royal Shopping centre. *(Hugh Llewelyn)*

Right: The town's other station, Windsor & Eton Riverside, opened in 1849 and originally served the Windsor, Staines & South Western Railway, and later the London & South Western Railway, the Southern Railway, British Railways and, currently, South West Trains. Designed by William Tite as a royal station for Queen Victoria, it is located near to the Thames and Windsor Castle. *(Hugh Llewelyn)*

country, and some of its 'brightest and blackest' pages are inseparably linked with the town. Its annals take us back to times when the rebellious Barons compelled King John, in its immediate neighbourhood, to sign the first great charter of our country's rights. York and Lancaster have each struggled for its possession. It has witnessed the extinction of royal houses, and sheltered within its walls the representative of England's short-lived Commonwealth. Within its precincts the Tudors have signed decrees to light the fires of Smithfield, and Cromwell has declared to Continental despotism, that no man shall be persecuted on account of his Protestantism. Great names, too, are associated with its annals, and he who has read the history of his country can pass in review, before his mind's eye, a long list of warriors, statesmen, churchmen, poets, and others, celebrated for their virtues or their talents, while he is also forcibly reminded that many names are mixed up with its history which he would willingly consign to oblivion.

The castle is divided into two courts, the upper and the lower, separated from each other by the Round Tower. On the north side of the upper court are situated the state apartments, and on the south the various apartments belonging to the officers of state. The lower court is chiefly remarkable as containing that beautiful structure St George's Chapel.

The Castle – The State Apartments are open on Mondays, Tuesdays, Thursdays, and Fridays, from 11 until 6. Tickets gratis, at Moon's, New Oxford Street; Colnaghi's, 14, Pall Mall East; Mitchell's, 33, Old Bond Street; Ackermann's, 96, Strand. Guide books may be had, from 1d to 1s. These tickets are available for a week from the day of issue, but not transferable; and no payment is to be made to the servants at the Castle. The private apartments are always closed, but a good panorama of their contents may be seen at Taylor's Illustrated Gallery, High-street, Windsor; admittance, 1s. Guide Books, 2d each. Choral service at St George's Chapel at 10 ½ and 4.

There is an ascent by the postern steps to the Castle for visitors arriving by the South Western rail; or you may go round to Henry VIII's gate, which leads into the town. It stands on a site of 12 acres, on the summit of a hill, commanding a magnificent view from the terrace, which is 1,870 feet, or 1/3 of a mile long. The great circular keep (open daily) from which the standard waves when the Queen is here, divides the upper and lower ward; it is about 150 feet above the quadrangle, or 300 feet above the park, and machicolated round the top, like most of the towers here. Twelve counties are visible in clear weather from the keep. Here state prisoners were confined. Since 1824 the resoration of the Castle, carried on by Sir Jeffry Wyattville has cost about £900,000. The state rooms, private apartments, etc are in the upper ward; St George's church, the deanery, apartments of the knights, baronets etc in the lower, as you enter from Henry VIII's gate.

The state apartments should be visited in the following order: - They are on the north side of the quadrangle.

Audience Chamber – Ceiling by Verro. Coronation of Esther, and the

Salter's Oxford and Kingston Steamer passing WINDSOR.

Above: Contemporary colour postcard of Salter's Oxford and Kingston steamer passing Windsor Castle, *c.* 1910. This Oxford-based company is still in existence. *(CMcC)*

Left: One of Brunel's lesser known bridges, the wrought iron 'bow string' bridge which carries the railway over the Thames. The Queen is reviewing the Fourth of June Eton procession on the river in 1889.

Lower left: The castle at Windsor has made the town a tourist must-see, and it was ever thus judging from this detail from a popular stereoscopic card from the end of the nineteenth century. *(LoC)*

triumph of Mordecai, in Gobelin tapestry; portraits of Mary, Queen of Scots, the 'daughter, consort and mother of kings,' as she is styled.

Presence Chamber – Charles II's queen, Katherine, on the ceiling. Subjects from Esther, in tapestry. Myten's portrait of George I's mother. Gibbon's carved work. Bacon's mantel-piece. This room is generally used as the ball room.

Guard Chamber – Old armour, including that of John of France (taken at Poitiers), and David of Scotland (captured at Neville's cross), both of whom were prisoners here in the reign of Edward III, who was born in the Castle, 1312. Also Henry, Prince of Wales, (son of James I), Prince Rupert's etc Chantrey's bust of Nelson, on a stand made out of the Victory's mast. Busts of Marlborough and Wellington (the latter by Chantrey), with the yearly banners presented to the Queen, on 2 August and 18 June, for Blenheim and Waterloo. Henry VIII's shield, by B. Cellini, the famous goldsmith.

St George's Banqueting Hall – 200 feet long, 34 feet broad; Gothic ceiling, full of escutcheons of the Knights of the Garter since 1350. Portraits of sovereigns from James I, by Vandyke, Lely, Kneller, etc. Throne, chair of state, etc in oak. Knights of the Garter are here knighted.

Ball Room – 90 feet long, by 34 broad; one fine Gothic window; furniture of the time of Louis XIV ('Louis Quatorze' style); Emperor of Russia's malachite vase; Jason and the Golden Fleece, in tapestry.

Throne Room – Carvings by Gibbons; ornaments of the Order of the Garter, in the ceiling and carpet; with portraits by Lawrence, etc.

Waterloo or Grand Dining Room is 98 feet long, and 45 high to the lantern ceiling. In the Elizabethan style. Full of portraits, etc of Waterloo men, sovereigns, and statesmen of that age; carvings by Gibbons; oak furniture; most of the portraits by Lawrence; among them are Picton, Anglesey, Wellington, Hill, Blucher, Castlereagh, Metternich, Pope Pius VI, Cardinal Gonsalvi (one of the best), Emperor Alexander, Platoff, Canning, and Humboldt.

Grand Vestibule, 47 foot long, 45 high, armour, banners etc.

Grand Staircase – Chantrey's statue of George IV.

State ante-room – Verrio's Banquet of the Gods, in the ceiling; tapestry, Gibbons' carvings; Reynolds' George III.

Small Vestibule, near the Waterloo Room. Large paintings by West, of the events in Edward III's reign. Carvings by Gibbons.

Rubens' Room – All paintings by Rubens, mostly life size, including his portrait by himself, his wife, Battle of Nordlingen, etc. Fine view from the Oriel; and chair made of wood from old Alloway Kirk.

Council Chamber of Charles II's time. Kneller's Duke of Marlborough, Lely's Charles II and Prince Rupert. Pictures by Flemish masters etc.

King's Closet, adorned with marine emblems. Quentin Matsys' misers and other pictures, Flemish, Italian, etc.

Queen's Closet – A small room with 'Adelaide Regina, 1853,' in the roof. Charles II and William III's silver tables. George IV's state bed. Portraits by Holbein, pictures by C. Lorraine, Teniers, etc.

Above: The east Terrace at Windsor Castle, showing the private apartments and ornate gardens complete with statues of elephants. *(LoC)*

Below: The classic view of the castle seen from the far bank of the Thames. *(CMcC)*

Queen's Drawing Room – Large pictures by Quccarelle.

Vandyck Room – Portraits by Vandyck of Charles I, his Queen, and family, Sir K. Digby, Duchess of Richmond, etc.

On the south and east sides of the quadrangle are the Queen's private apartments. In the middle is a bronze statue of Charles II with bas-reliefs by Gibbons.

St George's Collegiate Church, in the Lower Ward, was first built by Edward III, and rebuilt by George III. It is a long straggling cross in the decorated Gothic style, with battlements, buttresses etc, and a highly ornamented roof. The stalls and banners for the Knights of the Garter are in the choir. The windows are painted with subjects from West and Williment; that in the east window is the Resurrection by the former. There are various chapels and monuments; one of the oldest being that by Canon Ovenbridge, in 1522, near the cenotaph to the Princess Charlotte. In a vault near the fourth stall, Henry VI and Henry VIII are buried. (Henry VI was born in the Castle). Edward IV is also buried here under a curious tomb of iron work by Matsys; and George III and most of his family lie in the Tomb House or Mausoleum at the east end. George III's affectionate tablet to Mary Gaskoine, servant to his daughter Amelia, is in the cloisters.

There is a descent by the hundred steps to the town near the apartments for the Naval Knights. The Military Knights are lodged in the Lower Ward, they were established by Henry VIII and paid 1s per day. The Dean and Chapter were also allowed 1s per day out of the same fund; but while the emoluments of this body have been made to increase with the relative value of money, that of the Knights has remained the same.

The York and Lancaster gate, or main entrance to the Castle, fronts the Long Avenue. The Little Park is about four miles round. It contains Adelaide Lodge, at the bottom of the pretty slopes, the Royal Gardens; and Frogmore, the seat of the late Duchess of Kent; but Herne's Oak with 'great ragged horns,' to which the Merry Wives of Windsor inveigled Falstaff, disguised like Herne, with huge horns on his head, was cut down many years ago, though another tree has taken its name in Queen Elizabeth's walk.

From the Castle gate a noble avenue of tall spreading elms, three miles long, and nearly 300 foot broad, leading to the great Park, to Snow Hill, a low eminence surmounted by Westmacott's massive statue of George III, 66 feet high, including the pedestal. Cooper's Hill, Runnymede, and the Thames, Harrow Hill, etc are visible. Here the scenery becomes wild and forest like. The original Windsor Forest extended over 15 or 20 miles, almost to Reading. Near this is Cranbourne Lodge in the neighbourhood of the *Conqueror's Oak*, an ancient tree, nine or ten centuries old, 26 feet in girth and quite hollow. Queen Anne's, Queen Caroline's, Queen Charlotte's, Queen Adelaide's and Queen Victoria's trees are also seen, the last being bare for 50 feet from the root.

Eton College

Left: Nineteenth-century photograph showing the plainness of the furniture in one of the classrooms. *(NARA)*

Lower left: Britain's elite preparing for war. The Eton Rifles never existed as such – strictly speaking it is the Eton College Combined Cadet Force – but this term became universally used as a result of The Jam's 1979 single. Apparently it is a favourite song of Old Etonian David Cameron. *(Nationaal Archief)*

ETON

HOTELS – GREAT WESTERN; GEORGE; UPPER SHIP.

ETON is celebrated for its college, founded in 1440, by Henry VI, to which resort annually about 850 students, chiefly the sons of noble and opulent families. The triennial celebration of *Eton Montem* on Salt Hill, but now discontinued, the 'salt' or money, given to the captain of the school, for his support at the University, frequently realising nearly a thousand pounds. Passing over a neat bridge, which connects Eton with Windsor, the visitor will enter the town, associated with historical and literary reminiscences of the highest interest. We give a description of Windsor Castle in Section I, page 68.

The scenery around Windsor is remarkable for its sylvan beauty; and the weary citizen, who desires to enjoy a summer holiday, cannot do better than procure an admission ticket to Windsor Castle from the printsellers, Messrs Colnaghi, of Pall Mall, and then make his way to the Great Western Railway, in time for an early train. Within the next three hours he may see all the regal splendours of the palatial halls of Windsor; and then, having refreshed the inward man at any of the 'hostelries' which abound in that town, he may stroll forth into the country and contrast the quiet and enduring charms of nature with the more glittering productions of art, with which wealth and power surround themselves. He may walk in the shades of the forest, sung by Pope; he may saunter over Datchet Mead, immortalised by Shakespeare, in his story of Jack Falstaff and the buck-basket; or he may prolong his stroll to the quiet village of Horton, where Milton lived, and sang its rural charms in the immortal rhymes of 'L'Allegro' and 'Il Penseroso.'

Eton College, on the Bucks side of the Thames, was founded 1440 by Henry VI upon the plan of Winchester; its object being to supply King's College at Cambridge, as William of Wykeham's supplies New College at Oxford. Two brick quadrangles, in one of which is the founder's bronze statue, the chapel and upper school, built by Wren; and in the other the ancient Commons' Hall; the new buildings are in the Tudor style, the Chapel is Gothic, 175 foot long, with turrets at each corner. Bacon's statue (marble) of Henry VI is under the west window. A brass of Lord Gray (1521), deserves notice; the oldest is 1424. Sir H. Wotton and John Hales are buried here. Busts of Gray, Fox, Canning, etc, in the upper school, and other Etonians. Peel, the late Duke of Wellington, Chatham, Porson, are on the list. Album, with autographs of the Queen, Prince Albert, Louis Philippe, etc, in the library, which contains many books, MSS., curious maps, etc. A collection of portraits at the Provost's apartments.

At Salt Hill the *Eton Montem* used to be held every Whitsuntide, till 1847 when it was discontinued. Regatta on 4 June; boat races on the last Saturday in July, at Brocus Meadows. Further up the river, the Monkey Island, and a fishing temple built by the Duke of Marlborough.

Upton Church is a complete specimen of the Norman style, and contains the grave of Sir W. Herschel the astronomer, whose observations were carried on at Slough; but the great telescope, 40 foot long, is removed. At *Stoke Pogis* Church, and ancient building covered with ivy, *Gray* is buried; it was the scene of his beautiful Elegy in a Country Churchyard. In *Stoke Park*, the seat of the Penns, (descended from the founder of Pennsylvania), are some remains of an old house which belonged to Coke the great lawyer; portraits, etc, in the present mansion.

Down the river you come to Old Windsor or *Windlesford*, where the Saxon and early Norman kings fixed their seats at first; and *Ankerwyke*, the Harcourts' seat, where there is a famous oak, 33 foot girth, as old as the Conquest. Runnymede, which comes from the Saxon *Runeomede*, or Council-field, is near Charter Island, and is the spot on which the barons (fighting, however, for their own hand as the Scotch say), extorted the Great Charter from King John in 1215. *Ditton Park* is Lord Montague's seat.

Didcot

Above left: The station's all-over roof, shown in *Measom's Illustrated Guide to the GWR*, 1852.

Above right: A GWR Castle on the mainline at Didcot in 2010. *(Mertbiol)*

Right: GWR Diesel Railcar No. 22, now preserved at the GWR Society's Railway Centre at Didcot.

Bottom: No. 5051, built in 1936 as *Drysllwyn Castle*, renamed as *Earl Bathurst* the following year. Also at Didcot and photographed in 2005.

Didcot–Oxford Branch

DIDCOT (Junction)
A telegraph station.

MONEY ORDER OFFICE at Wallingford.

After passing a small and uninteresting village called Appleford, we come to a lofty embankment, from which some expansive and diversified views of the surrounding country are obtained. One mile further is the station of

CULHAM (Junction)
Distance from station, 2 miles.

A telegraph station.

MONEY ORDER OFFICE at Abingdon.

ABINGDON (Branch)
Telegraph station at Culham, 3 ¾ miles.

HOTELS – Crown and Thistle; Queen's Arms.

MARKET DAYS – Monday and Friday.

FAIRS – First Monday in Lent, 6 May, 20 June, 5 August, 10 September, Monday before Old Michaelmas Day, Monday after 12 October, and 11 December, for cattle and horses.

RACES in September.

A small parliamentary town in *Berks*, with about 5,680 inhabitants, returning one member. It is situated at the junction of the Wiltshire and Berkshire canal on the Thames, and the mouth of the river Ock, occupying a very favourable situation on the borders of Berkshire. The town consists of several wide streets, converging in a spacious area, where the markets are held every Monday and Friday. It takes its present name from a rich mitred abbey which was founded by the Saxon kings. Before that, it was called *Seukestram* or *Shrovesham*. Some traces of the abbey are seen at a brewery. Leland, who travelled the country as histographer to Henry VIII, states that it was then a magnificent building. Geoffrey of Monmouth died abbot here, 1417. Henry I, called Beauclerc, for his learning, was sent to this abbey by his father the Conqueror, to be educated.

The few buildings worth notice are St Nicholas' old church, a market house and county hall, of ashlar stone, the county bridewell, a grammar school founded in the sixteenth century, and Christ's hospital, an old cloistered building of the same date, founded by Sir John Mason, a native, and statesman of James I's age. Malting and sack-making are the chief employments. In Leland's time it 'stondeth by clothing,' like many other agricultural towns,

The broad gauge

When Brunel designed the Great Western Railway he determined that it would be the finest in the land. At a time before any standardisation of gauge he selected one of just over 7 feet, as compared with the 4 feet 8 inches of the northern railways which were based on the Stephensons' gauge which they, in turn, had adopted from the collieries in County Durham. The broad gauge, Brunel correctly argued, would give a smoother ride plus greater capacity for passengers or goods.

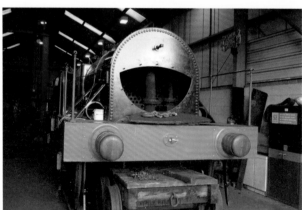

Top: This section of mixed gauge at Didcot graphically illustrates the difference between the two gauges' widths. *Middle left:* Also at Didcot, the replica broad gauge *Fire Fly* in the workshop. *Bottom:* The broad gauge graveyard at Swindon where the redundant locomotives awaited scapping.

The problem of incompatibility arose where the two gauges met – *as shown on page 54.* One solution was the transfer shed, such as the example at Didcot, *right*, which has a central platform between the two lines. In 1846 a Royal Commission came down in favour of the so-called 'standard gauge' because of its greater spread. The final stretches of broad gauge line were converted in May 1892.

Middle right: Another of Brunel's ill-fated experiments in traction, a section of atmospheric railway piping, on display at Didcot. A piston was pushed through the pipe by atmospheric pressure created by stationary steam engines, and was connected via the slot to the train. It was used on the South Devon Railway.

Below: North Star, a conventional broad gauge locomotive.

Culham

Brunel produced a standard design for smaller stations, and these became known as the 'Pangbourne type', *left*. Those on the mainline were lost when it was widened, but a fine example has survived at Culham on the line from Didcot to Oxford. It displays a wealth of characteristic Brunellian pseudo-Elizabethan detailing.

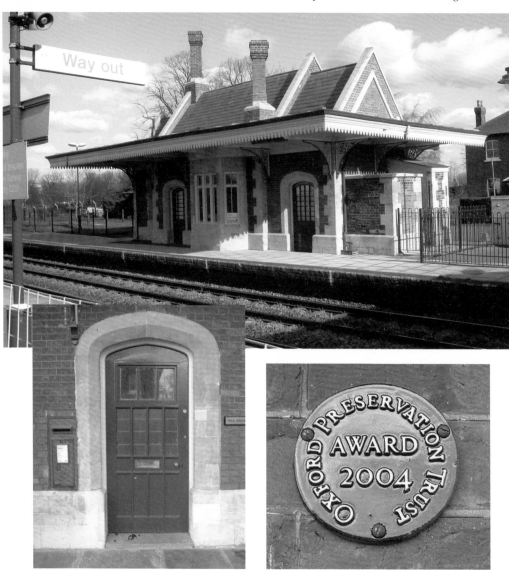

from which this important branch of manufacture has fled to the north, where machinery, coal, and other conveniences are more abundant.

OXFORDSHIRE

This rich midland county takes its name from the city of Oxford, and contains 481,280 acres, divided into 14 hundreds, and 219 parishes, and possesses one city, and twelve market towns. It is an inland county, founded on the east by Buckinghamshire, on the west by Gloucestershire. On the south-south-west and south-east its limits unite with those of Berkshire. The south-east part is hilly and woody, having a continuation of the Chiltern hills running through it; the north-west is also elevated and stony; and the middle is, in general, a rich country, watered by numerous streams, running from north to south, and terminating in the Thames. Of these the most considerable are, the Windrush, Evenlode, Cherwell, and Thame. The produce of this county is chiefly like that of most midland farming counties: much butter and cheese are made, and numerous calves are reared and fed for the London markets.

About three miles beyond Culham, we come in sight of Bagley Wood, seen to the left of the line, and soon after the little church of Sandford is observed peering through the trees to the right, and the Pauper Lunatic Asylum, a considerable pile of buildings, at Littlemore. A brief view of hills, a rapid glimpse of vallies, veined with pleasant streams, and studded with picturesque masses of woodland, a prolonged whistle from the engine, and a sudden whirl under a lofty, elegant portico, and we are at

OXFORD

POPULATION, 27,560.
DISTANCE FROM STATION, 1 MILE.
A TELEGRAPH STATION.
HOTELS – CLARENDON; MITRE; ROEBUCK.
FAIRS – 2 MAY, MONDAY AFTER ST GILES, 1 SEPTEMBER, AND THURSDAY BEFORE NEW MICHAELMAS.

OXFORD is the capital of the rich midland county of the same name, and one of the most ancient cities of England. It has for ages been celebrated for its university, which, in extent, number of its colleges, wealth of endowments, and architectural beauty, stands unrivalled by any similar institution in Europe; in fact, the period of its existence as a seminary for learning is supposed to date anterior to the time of Alfred. It is situated on a gentle eminence in a rich valley between the rivers Cherwell and Isis, and is surrounded by highly cultivated scenery – the prospect being bounded by an amphitheatre of hills. From the neighbouring heights the city presents a very imposing appearance, from the number and variety of its spires, domes, and public edifices; while

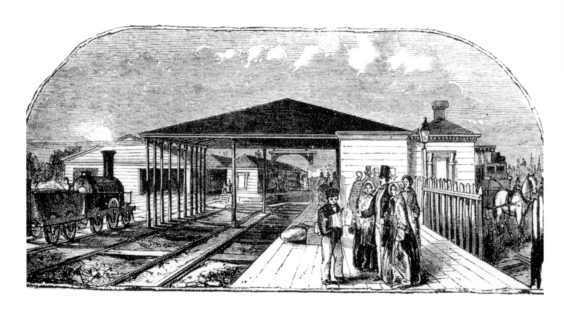

Oxford station

Above: The original wooden station building for Oxford was at St Aldate's and opened on 12 June 1844. The present station was brought into use in 1852 and the lower photograph dates from the Edwardian era, probably around 1908. *(Stanley C. Jenkins)*

these structures, from their magnitude and splendid architecture, give it on a near approach an air of great magnificence. The rivers are crossed by bridges. This city was distinguished by its attachment to the unfortunate Charles I, who here held his court during the whole civil war.

The High street extends east and west, under different names, the whole length of the city. From Carfax Church it is crossed, at right angles, by St Giles, the other principal street; and from these two branch off nearly every other street in the city. The High street of Oxford is justly considered the finest in England, from its length and breadth, the number and elegance of its public buildings, and its remarkable curvature, which, from continually presenting new combinations of magnificent objects to the eye, produces an uncommonly striking effect. There are also several other handsome streets of recent creation. Oxford has long been famous for good sausages and brawn. The 'Crown' is a small inn, entered from the Corn Market by a gateway. This inn was kept by the mother of Davenant, and was the resort of Shakespeare in his journies from London to Stratford-on-Avon.

Ye fretted pinnacles, ye fanes sublime,
Ye towers that wear the mossy vest of time;
Ye mossy piles of old munificence,
At once the pride of learning and defence;
Ye cloisters pale, that, lengthening to the sight,
To contemplation, step by step, invite;

Ye temples dim, where pious duty pays
Her hold hymns of everlasting praise –

Hail! Oxford, hail!

T. Warton's Triumph of Isis.

This venerable seat of learning has an advantage over Cambridge, in being placed among more attractive scenery, and combining in itself a greater variety of splendid architecture. It stands at the junction of the Cherwell and Thames, 63 miles from London by the Great Western railway, which is continued hence, on the broad or mixed gauge, to Banbury, Birmingham, Worcester, etc. The railway and the meadows round the city were all under water in the floods of 1853. Population, 27,850, who return two members to Parliament, while the University is represented by two more.

Distant prospects of the city may be obtained from the Shotover and Hinksey hills. It is called Oxeneford in Domesday Book, or the ford of oxen; and this homely interpretation is duly supported by the city arms. King Alfred, it is asserted, founded the University; but this appears to be doubtful, as his biographer, Asser, mentions nothing of it. Its pre-eminence is, however, admitted as a settled point by legal authorities. There was a nunnery (St

The city of dreaming spires

Two views of Oxford in the form of late-Victorian coloured Photocroms. These commercially produced images were created using printed colour tints. *Above:* Looking across the city of 'dreaming spires', a term coined by poet Matthew Arnold. *Below:* A more intimate view of Magdalen College seen from the river. *(LoC)*

Frideswide's) here from the year 730; and the monks attached to it, or to the monasteries founded after the Conquest, had the training of Henry I, who here acquired his surname of *Beauclerc*, from his literary parts.

Two mains streets, each about two-fifths of a mile long, cross at a market place, called Carfax, a corruption of *quatre voces* or four ways, where was a conduit, now at Nuneham Courtney, and contain in or near them some of the best buildings. High Street runs east and west, and St Giles' Street north and south. At one end (the east) of the former thoroughfare is Magdalene Bridge, by which the city should be approached, as from that spot a view may be obtained which is stated to exceed that of most other towns, by experienced travellers; it is curved, and the size, grandeur and variety of the buildings, as you turn through it, offer a most striking display. Another fine prospect may be had of the broad part of St Giles' Street, north of Carfax.

City Buildings – The best of these are – the *Town Hall* (built 1752), 135 feet long. The *Council Chamber* contains portraits of James II, the Duke of Marlborough, and others; the *Music Room*, built 1748, by an amateur architect, Dr Camplin; the *Infirmary*, founded by Dr Radcliffe; and the *County Gaol*, on the west side of the town. The last occupies the site of a castle founded after the Conquest, by Robert d'Oyley, and razed by Parliament, in the civil war, with the exception of the tower of St George. The *New Museum* in the Parks, though not pleasing externally, is one of the finest buildings of the kind in England. It was built from designs by Messrs Dean at the expense of the University, at a cost of £70,000. A new town has sprung up beyond the Parks.

Churches – *St Aldates*, or *Old's*, as it is called, is an old edifice near Christ Church, in the south quarter of Oxford. *St Cross* or Holywell, an ancient Gothic church, near the Cherwell; *All Saints*, in the middle of High Street, in the classic style, built by Dean Aldrich. *St Giles'* at the top of that street, is an early Gothic edifice; *St Michael's* near the bottom, and *St Martin's*, at the bottom, near Carfax, are two others. That of *St Mary Magdalene* is also a very ancient foundation, to which a new aisle was added in 1841, in honour of the martyrs Cranmer, Ridley, and Latimer, who were burnt (the last two in 1535, and Cranmer the year following) in Canditch, near Baliol College. Close to this church is the beautiful *Martyrs' Cross*, a three-storied Gothic pile, 73 feet high, by Scott. Statues of these celebrated Protestant confessors, by Weekes, are placed in the niches, and the whole lodged here in 1841, exactly three centuries after the publication of Cranmer's Bible. The famous Bocardo prison, in which they were confined, was in a gate of the old wall at the top of St Giles' Street. *St Mary's*, in High Street, is marked by a fine Gothic spire, 180 feet high; it is the University Church. *St Peter's* near Magdalene Bridge, is a restored Norman and pointed edifice. The *Cathedral*, part of Christ Church College, in Aldates Street. It was originally the Church of St Frideswide's Priory, and was made the seat of a bishop in 1542 by Henry VIII. The oldest portion is the Norman door; the fine early Gothic cloisters are 54 feet long – spire 144 feet high. Some quaint effigies are seen; one of Schmidt's old organs; a quaint and curious wooden shrine of the saint. *St George's*, in George Street, *St Phillip's* and *St James'*, in Park Town, a continuation of St Giles' Street.

University Buildings – There are nineteen colleges and five halls in Oxford, having about 6,000 members, and a total revenue of nearly £480,000.

ALL SOUL'S COLLEGE, in High Street, was founded 1437, by Archbishop Chichley; a Gothic front, 194 feet long, and two courts, with a chapel and library behind. A leather screen in the chapel; the library was built by the Codrington family. Archbishop Sheldon, Jeremy Taylor, Herrick the poet, and Backstone the lawyer, were of this college.

BALIOL COLLEGE, in Broad Street, was founded in 1282, by the Baliol family; old court and new chapel. Wickliffe was master of this college before he became professor of divinity, and John Evelyn was a member. An iron cross marks the spot where Ridley, Latimer, and Cranmer were burnt at the stake. A new wing of College buildings and a fantastic Chapel have of late years been built, from designs by Mr Salvin.

BRAZENOSE COLLEGE is on the site of Little University Hall, and had an immense brass knocker, or 'nose,' on its Tudor gate; founded 1509. John Fox, the martyrologist, Spelman, and several other antiquaries, were among its members. The Chapel has been restored by Mr Buckler, of Oxford.

CORPUS CHRISTI, in Merton Lane, founded 1527, by Bishop Fox, who projected the union of the Roses. His crozier, portrait, and statue are in the library. In the president's gallery are portraits of the famous seven bishops, Kew, Trelawney, etc, Hooker and Bishop Jewel were members.

CHRIST CHURCH, which includes the cathedral, in Aldates Street. It was founded 1525 by Wolsey, who built the largest of its three courts, about 260 feet square. In the tower over the front (380 feet long) is the 'Mighty Tom,'

Above: Early photograph of the rooftops with the late-eighteenth-century dome of the Radcliffe Camera, part of the Oxford University's Bodleian Library. *(CMcC)*

30

which weighs 12,000lbs. Every night at ten minutes past nine it strikes 101 stokes, that is as many as there are students on the foundation. Wolsey's Hall is full of portraits, and the library, of busts etc; while, for members it reckons Sir T. More, Bishop Atterbury, Sr South, Lord Mansfield, Robert Boyle, Sir P. Sidney, Locke, Camden, Ben Jonson, Canning, Peel, Gladstone.

EXETER COLLEGE, founded 1315, by the bishops of Exeter; the front, which has been modernised, is 220 feet long, many of the members are from the diocese of Exeter. One was Noy, who proposed the levy of ship-money to Charles I. A fine new chapel, in imitation of the Sainte Chapelle, Pairs, has been recently built, from designs by Mr Scott.

JESUS COLLEGE is chiefly used by the countrymen of the founder, Hugh Price, a Welshman; two courts. Portraits of Charles I (by Vandyke) and Elizabeth in the hall. Archbishop Usher and Beau Nash were members. Recently fronted from designs by Messrs Buckler.

LINCOLN COLLEGE, founded 1427, by the bishops of that diocese; two small courts. Archbishop Potter and John Wesley were members.

MAGDALENE, or as it is generally called *Maudlin* COLLEGE, is in High Street, and was founded 1448, by William of Waynflete. Two old courts and a third modern one, behind a front, 1,300 feet long; in which are an old and a new gate, and a beautiful pinnacle tower of the fifteenth century, 150 feet high. The president entertains the Sovereign at public visits. Queen Victoria and Prince Albert were here in 1841. In 1687, James II made his celebrated attempt to force the Romish divine, Farmer, into the presidency instead of Hough. The choir (men and boys) sing a Latin hymn on the top of the tower every May Day morning at five o'clock. Dr Renth, the late president, died in his ninety-ninth year, in 1856. Addison's walk is here, in the large and beautiful grounds, by the Cherwell. Among other members were Wolsey, Latimer, John Hampden, Hammond, Collins, the poet, and Gibbon. The new Grammar School (built from designs by Messrs Buckler) contains a magnificent carved oak roof. Some handsome stained glass has lately been placed in the College Chapel. The choral services are celebrated.

MERTON COLLEGE, in John Street, is the oldest, being founded in 1264, by Walter de Merton (in Surrey). Three courts; the most ancient part is Bishop Rede's library, built 1376. The chapel, the parish church of St John the Baptist, is nearly as old; and contains a new painted ceiling and some good brasses. The choral services (for which Oxford is famed) are more effective here than in any other Collegiate Chapel. William of Waynflete, Bishop Hooper, and Massinger, Sir R. Steele, and Duns Scotus, were members, as well as Bodley, founder of the Library. *St Alban's Hall* adjoins this college. Merton Grove is worth a visit.

NEW COLLEGE, is approached from Broad Street, and was founded by William of Wykeham, in 1379, for draughting his scholars from Winchester; good quadrangle, cloisters, and Gothic chapel, in which the founder's pastoral staff is kept. Good gardens, City Wall. Choral service celebrated.

The University
Oxford University consists of thirty-eight constituent colleges, and although there is no firm evidence of when it was founded, it appears to date back to the end of the eleventh century, which makes it the oldest university in the English-speaking world.

From top to bottom:
Magdalen, Christchurch, New College and Trinity. *(LoC)*

Reynolds painted the window, or rather gave the design for it; which Warton refers to in a complimentary couplet. Philpot the martyr, Bishop Ker, Sir H. Wotton, etc, were of this college.

ORIEL COLLEGE is in Merton Lane, founded in 1324, by Edward II, whose golden cup is here. Raleigh, Sandys, Butler, poets, Dr Arnold, and Archbishop Whateley, were members of this college. Dr Newman, Keble (author of the *Christian Year*), Charles Marriott, and other celebrated modern theologians, belonged to this college, *St Mary's Hall*, founded in 1383, is attached.

PEMBROKE COLLEGE, in Aldates Street, is a modern foundation, not older than 1724. It contains a quadrangle, oriel gate, and new hall, built 1849, in the Gothic style. Carew, the poet, John Pym, the orator of the Long Parliament, Archbishop Newcomb, Dr Johnson, Blackstone the lawyer, and Whitfield, were members.

QUEEN'S COLLEGE is in High Street, founded in 1340, in honour of Edward III's Queen, Philippa; two courts. Archbishop Potter, Henry V, Cardinal Beaufort, Wycherley, the poet, Bernard Gilpin, the 'apostle of the north,' and Jeremy Bentham, were members. *Edmund Hall* formerly belonged to Osney priory.

ST JOHN'S COLLEGE, in St Giles' Street, was founded 1555, by Lord Mayor White, and receives many scholars from Merchant Tailors' School. The chapel was part of a Cistercian college, founded by Archbishop Chichley; Laud's MSS in the library. Fine gardens. Archbishop Laud, and Bishop Juxon, were of this college. It contains a pastoral staff and has good choral services.

TRINITY COLLEGE, in Broad Street, founded 1555, by Sir T. Pope, a native of Deddington; two courts, one by Wren. In the chapel, very fine carvings, by Gibbons, and a picture of the Resurrection (after West) in needlework, portraits of Sir T. Pope and T. Warton, the poet, in the hall, where the fellows dine

UNTAXED, UNTROUBLED, UNDER
THE PORTRAIT OF THEIR PIOUS FOUNDER

and Warton's *Progress of Discontent.* Archbishop Sheldon, Chillingworth, Selden, Lord Somers, Lord Chatham, Warton, and others, were members of Trinity. Chillingworth was born at Oxford. Very fine gardens.

UNIVERSITY COLLEGE, in High Street. It was founded as far back as 1280, by William of Durham (though by some attributed to King Alfred); front 260 feet long, with two gates, carvings by Gibbons in the chapel. Of this college Archbishop Abbot, Bishop Ridley, Dr Radcliffe, and Sir W. Jones, were members.

WADHAM was founded in 1613, by Nicholas Wadham; court, Gothic chapel, timbered hall. Blake, Bishop Wilkins, Dr Kennicott, Sir C. Wren, and Dr Bentley were members. Bishop Wilkins was Warden when the Royal Society was founded – the first meeting was held at his house. Fine gardens.

City of domes

Above: Radcliffe Camera, with All Souls College to the right, in Radcliffe Square. Photographed from the tower of St Mary's Church, the University church, in central Oxford. *(Tejvan Pettinger) Below:* Not a true dome, but the end of the Sheldonian Theatre, which was completed in 1668 to a design by Sir Christopher Wren. It is named after Gilbert Sheldon, chancellor at the time, and is used for musical performances, lectures and university ceremonies. *(LoC)*

WORCESTER COLLEGE, in Beaumont-street, founded in 1714, on the site of Gloucester Hall.

What are called the University Buildings, as distinct from the different colleges, are those grouped together in Broad Street, in a handsome square, round the Radcliffe Library. Here are the schools (where lectures on divinity, medicine, etc are read), partly in the Gothic style. The *Bodleian Library*, founded in 1602, by Sir T. Bodley, contains nearly a quarter of a million of books, old, new, and rare MSS. Over this is the Picture Gallery, in which are portraits, busts, the Arundel marbles, specimens of natural history, etc. Convocation Room, and the *Theatre*, for public meetings, built by Archbishop Sheldon in 1669, from Wren's designs, though only 80 feet by 70, will hold 4,000 persons. The *Clarendon Printing Office* was built by Vanburgh. A new printing office is behind it, near the observatory, a large quadrangular pile, 250 feet by 290, built 1829. The *Radcliffe Library* –

You proud dome, fair learning's simplest shrine –

is a handsome building of 16 sides, 100 feet diameter, built 1749, by Gibbs, at the cost of Radcliffe, the physician; busts, marbles, books, and drawings are here. Its dome, thus alluded to by Warton, is one of the most conspicuous objects in the views of Oxford. In the *Ashmolean Museum*, which is nothing better than a large curiosity shop, are the head and feet of the famous *Dodo*, whose portrait is in the British Museum. The rest of him was destroyed as rubbish, by order, in 1755. One of the most complete accounts of this solitary specimen of a race which has become extinct in the present age of man, may be found under 'Dodo,' in the *Penny Cyclopoedia.*

In St Giles' Street stands the *Taylor Institute*, a handsome modern building in the Italian style, built by Cockerell. The centre is 150 feet long, and the wings 70. It is designed to be a complete gallery of arts and science. It is also a college for modern languages. Various drawings, paintings, busts, etc, are collected here. The *Botanic Garden* is fronted by one of Inigo Jones' gates.

Beaumont Street, near the castle, is so called after a palace built here by Henry I. Here Henry II lied, and his two sons, Richard of the Lion's Heart and John Lackland, were born. Another native was Anthony a Wood, the antiquarian, and the well known author of the *History of Oxford*, and of its eminent members.

North of the town, a little up the Thames, is Osrey Mill, on the site of an abbey formerly of great note. Not far from this stood Godstow nunnery, where Rosamund Clifford was wooed by Henry II. Fair Rosamond was a nun here, and was buried under the chapter house; her bones were scattered at the Reformation. The well known story of the bower in which she was concealed by Henry from his jealous queen, Eleanor, and the dagger and the cup of poison, is denied by critical historians.

A short line of 11 ¾ miles turns off to the left, passing the stations of

Blenheinm Palace, Woodstock
Designed by Vanburgh, Blenheim is the seat of the Duke of Marlborough and was given by Queen Anne and named after the great victory over the French in 1702. *Above:* Engraving of the front published in the *Vitruvius Britannicus* in 1725. The recent photo from the back of the building was taken almost 300 years later, in 2008. *(Jvhertum)*

Left: Blenheim's most famous son is Winston Churchill. Born on 30 November 1874, his full name was Winston Leonard Spencer-Churchill, but like his father he used the surname Churchill in public. Photographed in 1943, while he was Prime Minister, he is feeding Rota, a famously fierce lion at London Zoo. *(CMcC)*

YARNTON, EYNSHAM, and SOUTH LEIGH, to the town of WITNEY, celebrated for its manufacture of blankets.

OBJECTS OF NOTICE NEAR OXFORD

Blenheim, the Duke of Marlborough's seat, is the great attraction. It was part of the Manor of Woodstock, and was given to the great Marlborough, by Queen Anne, to commemorate the important victory over the French, of 2 August, 1702, on which day, every year, the holder of the seat presents a stand of colours to the queen. The house was built by Vanburgh, and is an excellent example of his heavy, but picturesque style; it is nearly 390 feet long; the way the chimneys are disposed is much admired. The interior is adorned in the style of that day, with rich tapestries, painted ceilings, etc. A piece of ornamental water in the parks, by 'Capability' Brown; also a pillar, 130 feet high, celebrating Marlborough's victories, the inscription being written by Lord Bolingbroke; and Rosamond's Well, which is all that remains of the White Castle, a bower, etc, the chief scene of Scott's Woodstock.

Warton's inscription on a spring here is pretty –

HERE QUENCH YOUR THIRST, AND MARK IN ME
AN EMBLEM OF TRUE CHARITY.
WHO WHILE MY BOUNTY I BESTOW
AM NEITHER HEARD NOR SEEN TO FLOW.

Woodstock Park was a favourite seat of King Alfred, and succeeding monarchs. Edward III's son, the Black Prince, was born here, in 1330; near the park gate stood a house in which Chaucer the poet resided. Good leather gloves are made at Woodstock. *Ensham* the seat of Lord Parke, and *Cornbury* that of Lord F. Churchill, are both near *Wychand Forest*, a well wooded tract of oak, beech and other timber, which is to be reclaimed and cultivated. Warton (who is poet of Oxford and the localities around) wrote some of his best lines, 'The Hamlet' here. Some rare fossils are found in the rock below, which is a soft shelly oolite. Stonesfield in particular, on the old Roman way or Wheman Street, has furnished valuable specimens, and a Roman pavement was discovered there in the last century. *Witney* (10 miles) is still a flourishing seat of the blanket manufacture. *Cumnor Place* (in Berkshire), which belonged to the abbots of Abingdon, was the scene, according to Scott's Kenilworth, of poor Amy Robsart's murder, by Verney, at the command of her husband, the Earl of Leicester. In the church, a marble effigy of Anthony Foster, who was implicated in the tragedy; but he is there described as a gentleman and scholar. The 'Black Bear' still figures at the village inn. *Nuneham Courtney*, on the Thames, is the seat of the Harcourts, at which are to be seen curious county maps, worked in tapestry, and a picture gallery.

ADLESTROP STATION   –)
THE PADDINGTON + WORCESTER EXP:
PASSING THROUGH –

Remember Adlestrop

Above: Immortalised in the poem by Edward Thomas, written in 1917 after his train had made an unscheduled stop, this Oxford, Worcester & Wolverhampton Railway station serves nearby Stow. *(Stanley C. Jenkins)*

Left: Moreton-in-Marsh has managed to reatain much of the character of a country station. The present buildings came after Brunel's time, but they are a fine example of the period and the pert signal box below is a welcome survivor.

The Old Worse & Worse

The Oxford, Worcester & Wolverhampton Railway

ADLESTROP AND STOW ROAD
Hotel – Unicorn.

Dalesford House, the seat of the celebrated Warren Hastings, and *Adlestrop House*, of the Leigh family, are close by. Stow-on-the-Wold, is a small market town on the summit of a hill, 883 feet high. The church, with its embattled tower 81 feet high, is consequently a prominent object through a circumference of many miles. It has many points and some curious monuments deserving attention.

Again proceeding on our way, we soon arrive at

MORETON-IN-THE-MARSH
Hotels – Unicorn, White Hart.

A small town on the old Foss Way; an old building once the Market House stands in the centre. In the vicinity are *Batsford* (3 miles), Lord Redesdale. *Seisincote* (2 miles), the four mile-stone (2 miles), where Oxfordshire, Glo'ster, Worcester, and Warwickshires unite, and where Canute was defeated by Edmund Ironside.

BLOCKLEY, CAMPDEN, and HONEYBOURNE stations, the last of which is the junction of the branch to the classic town of Stratford.

(STRATFORD-ON-AVON BRANCH – the Stations en route are LONG MARSTON, and MILCOTE.)

Honeybourne to Worcester and Wolverhampton.
Again on the Main Line, we next pay a visit to the small town of

EVESHAM
Distance from station ¼ mile. A telegraph station.
HOTEL – Crown.
MARKET DAY – Monday.
FAIRS – 2 Feb., Monday after Easter, Whit-Monday, 21 Sept.

This place has a population of 4,680, engaged chiefly in agriculture, with a little stocking and ribbon manufacture. It was remarkable for its mitred Abbey, founded by St Egwin in 709. The tower and gateway still remain.

FLADBURY station.

OWWR Locomotive
Above: No. 41, a large wheeled 2-4-0 loco. Built in 1855 for the OWWR, it became GWR No. 189 and is shown wearing that number on the cab in this photograph. *(Stanley C. Jenkins)*

Charlbury station
Below: Another example of a Brunel-designed station building. This 1912 photograph also shows a wooden goods shed, but both this structure and the later signal box has now gone. *(Stanley C. Jenkins)*

PERSHORE

Distance from station, 2 miles.
Telegraph station at Evesham, 5½ miles.
HOTEL – Angel.
MARKET DAY – Tuesday.
FAIRS – Easter Tuesday, 26 June, Thursday before All Saints, and 1 November.

The staple manufacture here is stockings. At this place the ruins of the Abbey House, the only relics of a large monastic establishment, may be seen. The situation of the town is very beautiful, and the surrounding scenery is picturesque, particularly Aylesborough, about a mile from the town.

WORCESTER

A telegraph station.
HOTELS – Star and Garter; the Hop Pole; the Bell; the Unicorn; the Crown.
MARKET DAYS – Wednesday and Saturday.
FAIRS – Saturday before Palm Sunday, Saturday before Easter, 15 August, 19 September, and the first Monday in December.
RACES in July and November.

WORCESTER, the capital of Worcestershire, in a fine part of the Severn, is a parliamentary borough (two members), and seat of a diocese, with a population of 31,227.

One distinct branch of manufacture is glove making, to the amount of half-a-million pairs of leather and kid gloves annually, employing between 1000 and 2000 persons. Another is boots and shoes; and the third is fine porcelain china, which was established here about a century ago by Dr Wall (the same who made the Malvern Waters known). Chamberlain and Grainger's are the two oldest.

The main streets, High Street, Foregate, and Broad Street, are well-built, broad and clean; and most of the houses of brick. Stone is abundant. A fine view from Froster.

Worcester, which the Saxons called *Weorgauceaster*, and similar names, being near the Welsh border, was provided with a fortress by the Conqueror. It was built by Urso d'Abitot, on Castle Hill; the county gaol occupies the site, built in 1819. No traces are left, nor of the city wall, which was erected at the same period.

The *Cathedral*, dedicated to St Peter, was formerly the church of a priory, founded by the Saxon kings. It stands on the south side of the city, between the river and the Birmingham canal. The oldest part dates from 1218, when it was rebuilt after a fire. The style, therefore, is early English, of a simple and unadorned character; the crypt, however, is Norman. It is shaped like a double cross, 384 feet long, and has a handsome tower, 170 feet high, so off by

Above: Worcester's Shrub Hill station which, at one time, had an all-over roof. The station has an impressive exterior and the platform level is raised up above a basement. *(Stanley C. Jenkins)*

pinnacles and statues in niches, especially that of St Wulstan. There is a well-carved bishop's throne, and an excellent organ. Music festivals are held here for the benefit of widows and orphans of clergymen, every third year, in turn with Gloucester and Hereford. That in 1788 was attended by George III, and the west window put in to commemorate his visit. The east window was finished in 1792. Another has been stained in memory of the late Queen Adelaide. Many interesting monuments are seen; among which, the oldest is King John's, whose body was shown to crowds of people in 1797, and replaced. Another ancient town is Lyttleton's, the lawyer (*Coke on Lyttleton*), who died in 1481; a Beauchamp, and two Crusaders, in effigy; Arthur, a son of Henry VII (whose widow, Katherine, was married to Henry VIII); the excellent Bishop Hough; the bas-reliefs, twelve in number, being some of the best works of the sculptor, Roubiliac; Bishops Gauden and Stillingfleet, the former the author of *Eickon Basilike, or the Image of a King*, which so much strengthened the sympathy for Charles I after his death, and several older prelates. In the Cathedral Precincts are the cloisters, 120 feet square, a Gothic chapter house, of ten sides, a copy of Rubens' *Descent from the Cross*, a King's College or School, founded by Henry VIII; and an old palace, from which there are good prospects. Portraits of George III and Queen Charlotte are here. There is another of the king in the Guildhall, in the market-place, a brick building, erected in 1723. It contains regal portraits of Charles I and II (with their statues), Queen Anne, and other personages, in the large hall, which is 110 feet long. The new Corn Exchange is here; Hop Market in Foregate. A theatre was built in 1780, and is 66 feet high. Handsome bridge across the Severn, built in 1781, on five arches. It has a fine view of the Malvern, Welsh, and Lickey Hills, and the beautiful fruit and hop country in the neighbourhood. In the Grammar School, founded by Queen Elizabeth, Lord Somers was educated: he was born here in 1650. Another student was S. Butler, the poet, a native of Strensham, near Pershore.

Of the twelve city churches, several deserve notice. *St Andrew*'s near the cathedral, is an early Gothic church, with a beautiful spire, built in the last century by a common mason; it is 155 feet high, and only 20 feet diameter at the bottom, where it rests on a tower 90 feet high. *St Peter's*, in Diglis Meadow, was originally built in the thirteenth century. Near this is the little harbour made by the junction of the canal with the river. Close to it are *St Alban's* and *St Helen's*, both very old churches. Across the bridge is *St Clement's*, a Norman copy of a former church. *St John's*, Bedwardine, is also half Norman.

There are several charitable institutions here, amply endowed, such as *Queen Hospital*, for twenty-nine women; *St Oswald's*, for twenty-eight women; *Judge Berkeley's*, for twelve persons; and the *General Infirmary* (near the Gaol and the Race Course), on Pitchcroft Meadow, founded in 1770. The various charities possess an income of £4,500 a year. A large *House of Industry* stands not far from the Gas Works. Near Sidbury Gate there stood not long ago part of a very old hospital whre the second Duke of Hamilton died of the wounds which he received in the famous *Battle of Worcester*, which was fought on 3 September, 1651, in Perry Wood, on Red Hill. Charles II, who was crowned here a little while before, occupied an old house (which is still standing) in *New Street*, from which he escaped by the back door, as the enemy pushed in at the front; and, accompanied by Lord Rochester and Father Hubblestone, his confessor, fled to White Ladies' Nunnery, at Boscabel. Cromwell styled this decisive battle his 'crowning mercy,' and named a ship, which was launched from Woolwich yard, the 'Worcester,' in consequence.

In the neighbourhood of Worcester are many other interesting spots:- *Bevere* (2 miles), supposed to have been a beaver colony, is a handsome seat on an island in the Severn, from which the Malvern hills are visible. Hither the citizens retreated during the plague of 1637, and it is frequented for bathing. *Perdiswell* is the seat of Sir O. Wakeman, Bart. *Claines* is near the remains of White Ladies' or Whitestone Nunnery, in which are preserved the bed and cup of Queen Elizabeth, who visited it in 1585. (This is distinct from White Ladies above mentioned). *Henlip* or *Hindlip*, the seat of Viscount Southwell, stands on the site of an old building in which Thomas Abingdon lived when he hid away some of the Powder Plotters in the secret passages which abounded it. It was the wife of this Thomas who wrote the anonymous letter to her brother, Lord Monteagle, which led James I to discover the plot. *Westwood Park*, near Droitwich, the fine old Elizabethan seat of

Three views of Worcester and its cathedral.

Top: Pleasure steamers on the river. *(CMcC)*

Below: The Promenade, and the Edgar Tower – an entrance into the College Green. This is a remnant of the old castle which had stood on the site since Norman times. *(LoC)*

Sir J. Pakington, Bart., fourth in descent (by the mother's side), from Sir Herbert Pakington, the 'Sir Roger de Coverley' of Addison. *Ombersley Park* belongs to Lord Sandys, a descendant of Sandys, the poet, and Archbishop Sandys; it contains many old portraits. *Hartlebury Castle*, near Stourport, the seat of the Bishops of Worcester for many centuries past; but most of it was rebuilt after the Restoration. *Hanbury Hall*, B. Vernon, Esq., an old seat. *Spetchley Park*, another old seat of the Berkeleys, now of R. Berkeley, Esq., their monuments are in the church. *Croome Park*, one of the largest in the county, is the seat of Earl Coventry, formerly of Urso d'Abitot. *Madresfield*, Earl Beauchamp's Court. *Boughton*, on the Teme, (which joins the Severn a little below the city), is the seat of J. W. Isaac, Esq. at *Hatton Park* there is a useful mineral spring, the property of J. Mann, Esq.

At *Upton* (9 miles), the celevrated Dr Dee, the astrologer was born. Near Malvern, in the direction of Upton, is a small but exquisitely built and decorated Roman Catholic chapel, and priest's residence.

COLWALL station.

DROITWICH JUNCTION
POPULATION, 7,086.
A TELEGRAPH STATION.
HOTEL – THE ROYAL.
MARKET DAY – FRIDAY.
FAIRS – FRIDAY IN EASTER WEEK, 18 JUNE, 24 SEPTEMBER, AND 18 DECEMBER.

DROITWICH is built on the banks of the river Salwarpe. It possesses a canal six miles in length, and capable of admitting vessels of 600 tons burden, and communicates with the river Severn. Its principal manufacture is that of fine salt, which is obtained by evaporating the water of brine springs, which are more than 100 feet below the surface of the earth.

HARTLEBURY
DISTANCE FROM STATION, 1 MILE.
TELEGRAPH STATION AT KIDDERMINSTER, 3 ¾ MILES.
MONEY ORDER OFFICE AT STOURPORT, 2 ½ MILES.

Here is situated Hartlebury Castle, for many centuries the residence of the Bishops of Worcester, which was reduced in the time of the Commonwealth, and rebuilt by Bishop Hough. The library of Bishop Hurd, together with some of Pope and Warburton's books, are at the castle.

KIDDERMINSTER
DISTANCE FROM STATION, 1 MILE.
A TELEGRAPH STATION.
HOTELS – LION, BLACK HORSE.
MARKET DAY – THURSDAY.
FAIRS – PALM MONDAY, HOLY THURSDAY, 20 JUNE, AND 4 SEPTEMBER.

Above: Photocrom view of the bridge over the Severn. If you look closely this is a colourised version of the same view shown at the top of page 44. *(LoC)*

Below: Two of the area's most celebrated exports. The composer Sir Edward Elgar was born in the village of Lower Broadheath, just outside of Worcester, in 1857. Known for his fine handlebar moustache, he also dashed off some good tunes including the *Enigma Variations* and the *Pomp and Circumstance Marches*. The latter was adapted for 'Land of Hope and Glory' and Elgar's music has come to epitomize the music of the Empire. *(LoC)* The other product is the celebrated Lea & Perrins' Sauce, usually referred to as Worcestershire Sauce to confound the Americans.

KIDDERMINSTER stands on both banks of the river Stour, which divides it into two unequal parts, and the buildings extend in a continued range from north to south-east, nearly a mile in length, and taken as a whole it forms a very regular and compact town, consisting principally of two good streets, one parallel to the canal, and the other forming part of the road to Birmingham. It returns one member. Population, 15,399. The church stands at the end of a street leading from the market-place, in a commanding situation, on the brow of a hill. It is a handsome Gothic building – the windows have very rich tracery, and the view of the town is uncommonly fine. There is a well-conducted and amply-endowed grammar school, founded by Charles the First. Kidderminster has long been celebrated for its manufactures, which are now on a very extensive scale, especially that of carpets, which has become very extensive, and has most essentially promoted the trade, wealth, and population of the town.

CHURCHILL station.

HAGLEY – Here is the splendid mansion of the first Lord Lyttleton; its picture gallery is attractive, and the scenery afforded by the situation of the hall itself beautiful and extensive. The family tomb may be seen in the church.

STOURBRIDGE
DISTANCE FROM STATION, 1 MILE.
A TELEGRAPH STATION.
HOTEL – TALBOT.
MARKET DAY – FRIDAY.
FAIRS – 29 MARCH AND 28 SEPTEMBER.

A handsome town, noted for its glass manufacture. Population 8,166. The surrounding districts abound in iron, coal, etc.

A line of 2 ¼ miles diverges from here to the right, *via* the station of LYE to the village of CRADLEY, in the vicinity of which some hops are grown.

BRETTEL LANE, BRIERLEY HILL, ROUND OAK, and NETHERTON stations.

DUDLEY
POPULATION, 44,975.
DISTANCE FROM STATION, ¼ MILE.
A TELEGRAPH STATION.
HOTELS – DUDLEY ARMS, BUSH.
MARKET DAYS – SATURDAY.
FAIRS – FIRST MONDAY IN MARCH, MAY, AUGUST, AND OCTOBER.

DUDLEY is a borough town in the county of Worcester. It received its name from a celebrated Saxon chieftain, who, as early as the year 700, built the Castle which commands the town.

OLD HEADSTONES, ST. JOHN'S CHURCHYARD, BROMSGROVE

Above: Not strictly within the remit of this book, these headstones at St John's churchyard in Bromsgrove are too topical to ignore. Featuring very early steam locomotives they mark the deaths of Joseph Rutherford and Thomas Scaife, two employees of the Birmingham & Gloucester Railway who lost their lives when the boiler of their steam locomotive exploded at Bromsgrove on 10 November 1840. Such boiler explosions were not uncommon on the early railways. *(CMcC)*

The night view from Dudley Castle of the coal and iron districts of South Staffordshire reminds the spectator of the Smithy of Vulcan, described by Homer. The lurid flames that issue from the summits of the huge columnar chimneys light up the horizon for miles around, and impart to every object a gloomy aspect. On whichever side the view is taken in open day, the evidences of mining industry present themselves, in the vast number of smoking, fiery, and every active works, which teem in this part of South Staffordshire. Taking Dudley Castle as a centre, we have to the north, Tipton, Gornal, Sedgley, Bilston, Wolverhampton, Willenhall, and Wednesfield. More easterly we find Great Bridge, Toll End, Darlaston, Wednesbury, West Bromwich, and Swan Village, which is a similar group to the former, and marked with precisely the same features – mining perforations, red brick houses, and black smoke. Turning towards the south, we find the iron towns fewer and wider apart, and lying, as it were, confusedly in four counties – Birmingham, for instance in Warwickshire; Smethwick, Dudley Port, Rowley Regis, Wordsley, and Kingswingord in Staffordshire; Oldbury, Hales Owen, Dudley, and Stourbridge, in Worcestershire. So singular, indeed is the intersection of these four counties that in going from Birmingham to Dudley Castle, by way of Oldbury – a distance of about eight miles by coach-road – we pass out of Warwick into Staffordshire, thence into Worcester, and a third time into Staffordshire, for although Dudley town is in Worcestershire, Dudley Castle and grounds are in Staffordshire. These several towns belong to the mining and manufacturing district, known by the name of the South Staffordshire *coal field* district, because it has a layer of coal running, so far as is known, beneath its surface.

Dudley Castle belongs to Lord Ward, who is also proprietor of a considerable portion of Dudley and its mines. It is situated in a large and highly picturesque park; and, with its warders' watch and octagon towers, triple gate, keep, vault and dungeon, dining, and justice halls, and chapel, though in a state of dilapidation, must be considered as a fine old ruin. The view from the summit of the keep is wide-spreading and singularly interesting; to the east, the busy hive of Birmingham; whilst to the south-west, nature has formed the Malvern Hills. These objects are all visible, and form an interesting background to the environs of Dudley.

As the eye sweeps the horizon from the summit of the keep, to discern the precise character of each object and locality, the mind is struck with one particular fact, that almost every town, village, house, man, woman, child, every occupation and station, are more or less dependent on, and are at the mercy of, lumps of coal and iron, and that the human race will mainly owe their moral regeneration to these two materials. The miner digs, the roaster calcines, the smelter reduces, the founder casts, the blacksmith forges, and the whitesmith files; these are but parts of the vast hive, whose busy hum of industry is heard far and wide, and whose skilful handiworks find a ready reception in every quarter of the globe. Leave Birmingham to itself, and direct your eye to West Bromwich – which has sprung up as it were but yesterday – and there you will perceive the best *puddlers* at work – the converters of pig-iron into its barred state – by far the most important of all the processes in the manufacture of that metal. Wolverhampton, Wednesbury, Bilston, and Dudley, have each their respective industries, and carry the division of labour to the minutest degree. Bloxwich, is almost exclusively employed in making awl-blades and bridle-bits; Wednesfield keeps to its locks, keys, and traps; Darlaston its gun-locks, hinges, and bolts; Bilston its japan-work and tin-plating; Sedgley and its neighbourhood, its nails; Willenhall its locks, keys, latches, curry-combs, bolts, and grid-irons; Dudley its vices, fire-irons, nails, and chains; Tipton its heavy iron-work; while Wolverhampton includes nearly all these employments in metal work. Looking further south, there may be descried Oldbury, Smethwick, Rowley Regis, Hales Owen, and Stourbridge – all of which are engaged in some form or another, in the manufacture of iron. We have not space to enlarge upon these facts, which are only a few in the vast multitude that are comprised in the area over which the view from the Castle extends, and therefore must content ourselves with laying a single one before the reader. The quantity of cast-iron produced throughout England and Scotland in 1851, amounted to nearly three millions of tons, and the share in that production by this district may be estimated at about one-third of that quantity, or five millions in value. Assuredly this limited area presents the most remarkable concentration of industry of which the world can boast.

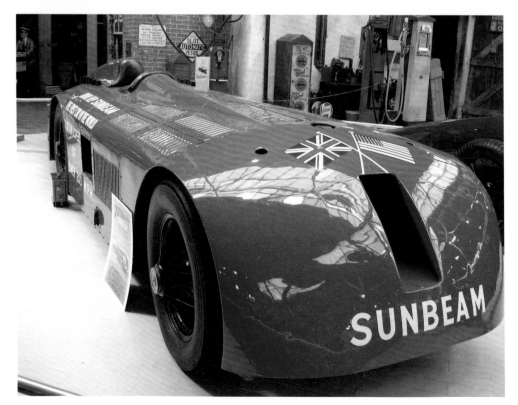

Above: The Wolverhampton Art Gallery. *(G-Man)*

Wolverhampton

Writing of nineteenth-century Wolverhampton, the Bradshaw guide tells us that 'all kinds of iron, brass, tin-plate, japan work, etc, are made here, as locks and keys, hinges, fenders, coffee mills, tea trays, bolts, files, screws, and other tools, besides engines, etc.' He doesn't mention the fledgling bicycle industry which grew to prolific proportions with 200 manufacturers in the area at one time. From these grew the local car manufacturers, including Sunbeam who produced a range of cars and, notably, the record-breaking Sunbeam 1000hp – known as *Mystery* or 'The Slug'. Powered by two aircraft engines, in 1927 it became the first car to exceed the 200 mph mark in the hands of Henry Segrave. It is now on display at the motor museum in Beaulieu, Hampshire, sharing the spotlight with Sir Malcolm and Donald Campbell's Bluebird cars. *(David Hunt)*

WOLVERHAMPTON

A TELEGRAPH STATION.

HOTELS – THE SWAN; STAR AND GARTER.

OMNIBUSES TO AND FROM BRIDGNORTH (CROWN HOTEL), DAILY.

MARKET DAY – WEDNESDAY.

FAIR – 10 JULY, LASTING THREE DAYS.

BANKERS – WOLVERHAMPTON AND STAFFORDSHIRE BANKS, OLD CHURCH YARD; BILSTON DISTRICT BANK, COCK STREET; MESSRS HOLYOAKE AND CO'S BANK, COCK STREET; MESSRS FRYER'S BANK, LICHFIELD STREET.

This ancient town, which in Saxon times was noted for its college, founded by Wulfruna, sister of King Egbert, and thence called *Wulfrunes-hampton*, from which it derives the modern name, is now a parliamentary borough (two members), and the capital of the *iron trade*. By the North Western, or narrow-gauge line, it is 126 miles from London (or 13 miles from Birmingham); by the broad gauge, *via* Oxford and Worcester, 142 miles. The branch covers about 30 square miles of barren soil, beneath which are rich crops of coal, iron, and stone. Population 147,670. All kinds of articles in iron, brass, tin-plate, japan work, etc, are made here, as locks and keys, hinges, fenders, coffee mills, tea trays, bolts, files, screws, and other tools, besides engines, etc. Smelting-houses and foundries abound on all sides (see *Bradshaw's Hand-Book to the Manufacturing Districts*). The making of tin-plate, that is, of iron tinned over, is a staple business. That of japanning was first introduced by Baskerville, the Birmingham printer, whose portrait may be seen in the counting-house of Messrs Longman, in Paternoster Row.

Wolverhampton stands on high ground, and has never suffered from the plague, but it did not escape the cholera in 1849, though the deaths were few compared with those at Bilston and Willenhall. The houses are of brick, and there are not any remarkable edifices. The *Grammar School*, founded in 1513 by a native, who became lord mayor of London, is well endowed, and replaces a hospital built by the Leveson or 'Luson' (ancestors of the Gower) family. There is a literary institute with a public library.

Of its eight churches, St Peter's is the most ancient and striking. It is a later English cross, having a tall tower and carved stone pulpit, with monuments of the Levesons, and of Colonel Lane, who, with his sister, were the means of effecting the escape of Charles II, after the battle of Worcester, 1651. It was that officer who was hid away with the king in the Royal Oak. A pillar cross in the churchyard in 20 feet high. Until lately, the manor belonged to the Dean and Chapter of Windsor, to whom it was granted by Edward IV.

Left: Queen Victoria came to Gloucester station in 1849. Unfortunately, because of the break in gauge, even she had to change trains. *See page 54.*
Below: Broad gauge replica at the Gloucestershire Warwickshire Railway in Toddington.

Left: Gloucester docks with the cathedral in the background. It dates back to the seventh century and is the resting place of Edward II, who was murdered at the nearby Berkeley Castle.

Gloucester & Cheltenham

[CHELTENHAM ON THE GLOUCESTER TO BIRMINGHAM LINE]

GLOUCESTER

POPULATION, 16,512.

A TELEGRAPH STATION.

HOTELS – KING'S HEAD, W. CHURCHILL; FIRST-CLASS FAMILY AND COMMERCIAL, HIGHLY RECOMMENDED AS A MOST COMFORTABLE HOUSE, IN THE CENTRE OF THE TOWN. BELL AND WELLINGTON.

MARKET DAYS – WEDNESDAY AND SATURDAY.

FAIRS – APRIL 5TH, JULY 5TH, SEPT. 28TH, AND NOV. 28TH.

BANKERS – COUNTY OF GLO'STER BANKING CO.; GLO'STERSHIRE BANKING CO.; NATIONAL PROVINCIAL BANK OF ENGLAND; THOMAS TURNER.

A cathedral city, capital of the county, and parliamentary borough (two members), on the Severn, and the Bristol and Birmingham Railway, 114 miles from London, in a flat spot, which was under water in the floods of 1853. At Kingsholme, to the north, on the site of a Roman station, called *Glevum,* the later Saxon kings had a seat, which, Canute attempting to take, was defeated, in the battle of Alney Island, close by. Laxington and other pleasant hills overlook the vale of Gloucester, a rich loamy tract of 60,000 acres, where considerable corn, fruit, beans, turnips, and hay are raised, though much of the butter and double Gloucester cheese, for which the county is noted, comes from the Wiltshire meadows. The corn market is held every third Monday, from July to November.

This town is situated on an eminence, in that division of Gloucester called the vale, near the banks of the Severn, and when viewed from that river it presents a very imposing appearance. The city possesses many elegant public buildings, and a magnificent cathedral, which is particularly celebrated for its architectural beauty. The *Cathedral* is a cross, 426 feet long; the oldest parts are the Norman crypt and nave, built in 1089. The later English choir is the work of Abbot Wigmore (about 1330), and a 'whispering' passage, 75 feet long, near the fine east window, which is 79 feet long by 35 broad, or one of the largest in England. The west front was built in 1437; the tower, which is 225 feet high, was begun a little later, but not finished till 1518; the Lady Chapel, 92 feet long, is the most modern part. There is a very old tomb of Edward II, (who was murdered at Berkeley Castle), also monuments of Robert Curthose the Conquerer's brother, and *Dr. Jenner,* the discoverer of vaccination. Some of the Lacy family are buried in the Chapter House. The beautiful cloisters were built between 1351 and 1392. Of the twelve churches, those of St. Catherine and St. Mary de Lode are Norman in part, and St. Nicholas is early English. At St. John's is a tablet to the Rev. T. Stock, who with *Raikes* established the 'four original *Sunday Schools* in

The break of gauge

Gloucester was one of the first points where Brunel's broad gauge met the narrower gauge – later to become the standard gauge – coming from Birmingham. As the two gauges were incompatible all goods and passengers, even horses, were required to transfer from one train to another in order to complete their journeys. The disruption this caused made Gloucester the rallying point for the anti-broad lobby and these illustrations from *The Illustrated London News* convey the ensuing chaos. 'In the hurray bricks are miss-counted, the slates chipped at the edges, the cheeses cracked, the ripe fruit and vegetables crushed an spoiled; the chairs, furniture, oil cakes, cast-iron pots, grates and ovens all more or less broken ...' Clearly this situation couldn't continue. *See also page 22.*

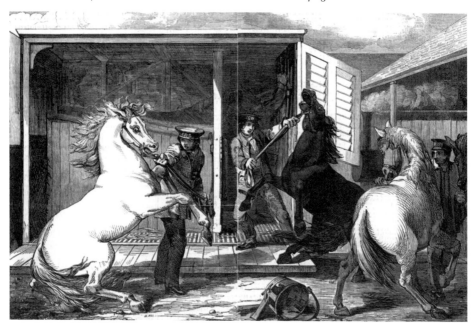

this parish and St. Catherine's, in 1780.' From this small beginning sprung that gratuitous system of Christian instruction which has covered the face of England and Wales with schools. Gloucester boasts another evangelist in *Whitfield,* who was born at the Bell Inn, while Bishop Hooper, whom it enlisted in the noble army of martyrs, was burnt in St. Mary's Square. Close to the rail and the ship canal basin is the County Gaol (on the castle site), where the separate system was first tried, 1790. Shipping come up to this basin by a cut from the Severn, near Berkeley; there is a good import trade. In this part also are the *Spa Gardens* and pump room, over a mineral spring of some value. The Shire Hall was built by Smirke; the Infirmary covers a space of seven and a half acres. In Commercial Street is a *Museum,* the gift of the Guises of Elmore Court. Pins are made here.

In the environs are the gate of Lanthoney Abbey, *Highnam Court,* seat of T. G. Parry, Esq., in the renaissance style; Churchdown, a solitary hill, having the Cots Wolds to the right, from 800 to 1100 feet high; Cheltenham and its mineral waters; Hempstead Harwick, Painswick, and other seats; Newent old priory; *Flaxley Abbey,* seat of Sir M. Boevey, Bart; the Forest of Dean, an interesting hilly wooded tract, stretching to the Wye, and producing iron, coal, stone, etc.; Ross, and its spire, built by Kyrle, the 'man of Ross,' overlooking the Wye, the beautiful scenery of which may be visited from here, as well as the Malvern hills, with the Hydropathic establishments of Drs. Wilson and Gully. *Goodrich Court,* seat of the Meyricks, near Ross, which has a remarkable collection of armour, etc., and is near a fine old Norman castle of the Pentroches.

Distances of places from the station

	Miles		Miles
Badgworth	3	Longford	1½
Barnwood	0½	Maizmore	3
Brookworth	3	Quedgeley	3
Churchdown	2½	Rudford	1
Elmore Court	5	Sandhurst	3
Forton	3	Studgrive	2
Hatfield Court	5	Upton	3
High Grove	3	Whaddon	3
Highnam Park	4	Wooten	1

CHELTENHAM.
   POPULATION, 39,693.
   A TELEGRAPH STATION.
   HOTELS – THE PLOUGH, FIRST CLASS, FOR FAMILIES AND PRIVATE GENTLEMEN; THE QUEEN'S, FIRST-CLASS, FOR FAMILIES AND GENTLEMEN. COMMERCIAL HOUSES, THE FLEECE AND THE LAMB.
   MARKET DAY – THURSDAY.
   FAIRS – SECOND THURSDAY IN APRIL, 2ND THURSDAY IN SEPT., HOLY THURSDAY,

Cheltenham

Left: A Military Fete and Flower Show at Pittville Spa, from an engraving published in *The Illustrated London News.*

Below: The gardens and footbridge at Pittville Park, which was opened in 1825. *(LoC)*

Left: Postcard view of the promenade gardens in Cheltenham, *c. 1905.*

BANKERS – Branch of Glos'stershire Banking Co.; National provisional Bank of England; County of Glo'ster Bank.

CHELTENHAM takes its name from the river Chelt, and is celebrated for its medicinal waters. It has been for the last sixty years one of the most elegant and fashionable watering places in England. The town is built on a flat marshy soil, on the borders of a rich and fertile valley, and the surrounding Leckhampton hills protect it from the cold winds. The season for drinking the waters is from May to October. The climate in winter is generally mild, though in July and August the heat is felt to be oppressive. Its surface is elevated about 165 feet above Gloucester, and the funnel shape of the valley, with a large river in its centre (the Chelt, which runs through to the Severn), elicits currents of air, which ventilate the atmosphere, and contribute much to the purity and salubrity of the town.

It is a parliamentary borough (one member), situated in a charming spot under the Cotswold hills, in Gloucestershire, 7 miles from Gloucester, on the Bristol and Birmingham Railway. Most of it is modern and well-built. The assembly rooms are in High Street, ¾ mile long. A little on the one side is the *Pittville Spa* and Pump Room (built in 1824), with its Grecian portico and dome, in the midst of pleasing grounds. On the other, the promenade leads to *Montpellier Spa* and *Rotunda* pump-room, and Lansdowne Crescent. A pump-room, built in 1803, stands at the *Old Wells*, first used in 1716, and approached by an avenue of elms, an object of deserved attraction, from its extent and symmetry. There is also the Chalybeate Spa. Both contain asperient salts of soda and magnesia, with a little iodine and iron; and are of great benefit in cases of weak stomachs, liver complaints and plethora. Two are chiefly chalybeate. The peaks and gardens about the town have much picturesque beauty, and are open throughout the year for a trifling fee, besides being the scene at intervals of numerous fetes and floricultural shows.

A *Proprietary College*, in the Tudor style, was built in 1843, 240 foot long. The parish church of St. Mary is in part as old as the 11th century. Christ church and St. Peter's, among the modern ones, deserve notice – the latter being in the Norman style, with a round tower, &c.

In 1831, Mr. Gurney tried his locomotive carriages along the high road to Gloucester, running the distance in 55 minutes, several times a day.

In the neighbourhood are many good walks and points of view, viz., Battledown, Leckhampton Court, and Clerk Cloud, 1,134 feet high. Behind Leckhampton are the *Severn Springs*, one of the principal heads of the river Thames. *Southam* is the Tudor seat of Lord Ellenborough. *Boddington Manor*, J. Neale, Esq. Charlton Park, &c. &c.

Ross-on-Wye

Left: The Hereford, Ross & Gloucester Railway opened on 1 June 1855. The railway was amalgamated with the GWR in 1862. This engine shed on the edge of the town is all that remains from the station at Ross. Built in 1871 it is post-Brunel, but nonetheless it is a fine structure. It now serves as premises for a garden centre.

Above: The Market House in Ross is now a visitors' centre.

Left: The coming of the railway to the town is illustrated in this contemporary engraving. The broad gauge line ran for just over twenty-two miles, connecting Hereford and Gloucester via the mainline junction at Grange Court.

Gloucester, Ross, Hereford

LONGHOPE (late Hopebrook).

DISTANCE FROM STATION, 1 MILE.

TELEGRAPH STATION AT GLOUCESTER, 11½ – RAILWAY.

MONEY ORDER OFFICE AT NEWENT.

MITCHELDEAN ROAD STATION.

ROSS.

TELEGRAPH STATION AT HEREFORD, 12¼ MILES.

HOTELS – ROYAL; KING'S HEAD.

MARKET DAY – THURSDAY. FAIRS – THURSDAY AFTER MARCH 10TH, ASCENSION DAY, JUNE 21ST, JULY 20TH, THURSDAY AFTER OCTOBER 10TH, DECEMBER 11TH.

BANKERS – J. W. R. HALL; MORGAN & CO., PRITCHARDS AND ALLAWAY.

Ross has a population of 3,715; is situated on a rocky elevation on the east bank of the Wye. In the church are several monuments of the Rudhall family, one of whom opposed Cromwell in his siege of Hereford. There is also one of Mr. J. Kyrle, the celebrated 'man of Ross', who was interred here. From the churchyard are some very beautiful views. Ross has great attractions during the summer months. *Goodrich Court*, the seat of Sir S. R. Meyrick, in the neighbourhood, is visited for its armoury. It may be seen on application.

FAWLEY station.

HOLME LACEY.

MONEY ORDER OFFICE AT HEREFORD.

This is the ancient seat of the Scudamore family, now in the possession of Sir E. F. Scudamore Stanhope, Bart. The mansion and grounds excite much interest, having a good picture gallery, and a giant pear tree, covering a quarter of an acre. Here Pope wrote the 'Man of Ross'.

HEREFORD

A TELEGRAPH STATION.

HOTELS – CITY ARMS, GREEN DRAGON.

MARKET DAYS – WEDNESDAY AND SATURDAY.

FAIRS – TUESDAY AFTER CANDLEMAS, EASTER WEDNESDAY, MAY 19TH AND 28TH, JULY 1ST, AND OCTOBER 20TH.

BANKERS – NATIONAL PROVINCIAL BANK OF ENGLAND; HEREFORD BANKING CO.; MATTHEWS AND CO.; HOSKINS AND MORGAN.

Hereford

Above: On Easter Monday 1786 the cathedral suffered a catastrophic collapse when the west tower fell, leaving the whole of the west face in ruins. Restoration work commenced in 1841 and the cathedral reopened in 1863, the same year that the *Bradshaw Guide* was published. The west front was not restored until the beginning of the twentieth century. *Below:* Herefordshire cattle with white faces and red coats. *Right:* The *Mappa Mundi* which is now housed in a new library building on the Cathedral Close.

 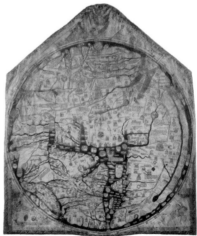

HEREFORD, the capital of Herefordshire, and a parliamentary borough, on the Shrewsbury and Hereford, Newport, Abergavenny, and Hereford, and Hereford, Ross and Gloucester lines. By rail, *via* Gloucester, the distance from London is 144¼ miles, but the distance by road is only 134, or 33 beyond Gloucester. Population, 15,585.

Hereford, as its old Saxon name explains it to be, stands at a *military Ford* on the Wye, which King Harold protected by a castle, the site of which, at castle Green, is now occupied by the Nelson Column, where an old bridge of the fifteenth century crosses the river a little higher. To this castle the barons brought Edward II's favourite, De Spenser, and executed him in 1322; and four years later the unfortunate king himself was here deprived of his crown. Parts of the town are low and old fashioned. Some remains of the old town walls are still visible. The soil without is a rich tract of meadow, orchard, and timber; and the internal trade is chiefly in agricultural produce, good cider and perry (which require a little brandy to qualify them), wool, hops and prime cattle – the last being a splendid breed, white-faced, with soft reddish brown coats. A few gloves and other leather goods are made. Salmon are caught.

The present Cathedral, lately restored, standing near the river, and dedicated to St. Mary, is the third on this site, the first one having been founded in the ninth century by King Offa, to atone for the murder of Ethelbert. It is a handsome cross, 325 feet long, begun by Bishop Herbert de Loxinga in 1079, when the Norman style prevailed, and finished by Bishop Borth in 1535, who built the beautiful north porch. The west front was spoiled by Wyatt, in restoring it after the fall of the tower above in 1786. There are two other Norman towers, and a great tower, which firmly support a tall spire. Some of the Gothic side chapels, and the monuments of Bishop Cantilupe, Bishop de Bethune, &c., deserve notice. A curious Saxon map of the world is in the library. The college of the Vicars-Choral, and the grammar school are in the cloisters; the latter was founded here in 1385.

The triennial music festivals are held in the *Shire Hall*, a handsome building, by Smirke, built in 1817. Near this is an ancient *Town Hall*, constructed of carved timber, 84 feet long, by 34 broad, of the time of James I, and resting on an open arcade, where the market is held; John Able was the builder. The county gaol, on the road to Aylestone Hill, is on the site of a priory, founded by the De Lacys; the infirmary, near the castle Green. At the opposite end of the town, past Above Eign, is the *White Cross*, built in 1347, to serve as a market for the country people when the town was ravaged by the plague. Near the bridge and the old palace is the preaching cross of the Black Friary. All saints Church and St. Peter's are both Norman, though altered by late restorations. The tower of All saints leans seven feet from the perpendicular. St. Martin's is a new Gothic church, in place of one ruined by the royalist party. Poor *Nell Gwynne* was born here.

In the neighbourhood are various points of interest. Up the Wye are – Belmont; Sugwas, once a country seat of the bishops; *Garnons*, Sir G. Cotterell Bart., in a fine spot, under Bishopstone Hill; *Moccas*, Sir V. Cornewall, Bart., in an immense park. *Sufton Court* is the seat of the Herefords, an ancient family. *Hampton Court*, the old seat of the Coningsbys, belongs to – Arkwright Esq., a descendant of the great cotton spinner. *Foxley*, Sir R. Price, Bart., was planned by Price, who wrote the 'Essay on the Picturesque,' according to the principles laid down in that work. Leominster, a parliamentary borough, has many old timbered houses, especially one built by the architect of Hereford Town Hall.

Melksham and Bradford on Avon

Above: Postcard of the railway station at Melksham, *c.* 1905. Opened in 1848, it is on the branch line from Chippenham to Trowbridge, originally part of the Wilts, Somerset & Weymouth Railway which was absorbed by the GWR in 1850. *(CMcC) Below:* Bradford on Avon's famous Town Bridge and lock-up, where trouble-makers were put for the night.

Wiltshire & Somerset

WILTS, SOMERSET & WEYMOUTH RAILWAY

MELKSHAM

DISTANCE FROM STATION, ¾ MILE.
A TELEGRAPH STATION.
HOTEL – BEAR, KING'S ARMS.
MARKET DAY – MONDAY.
FAIRS – 27 JULY, AND THE SECOND MONDAY IN EVERY MONTH.
MONEY ORDER OFFICE.
BANKERS – THE NORTH WILTS BANKING CO.

This village has a population of 4,251; consists of one long street, the buildings of which are mostly of freestone. Celebrated for its mineral springs.

DEVIZES BRANCH

Melksham to Devizes

This branch, also an appendage of the Wilts, Somerset and Weymouth line, turns off about a mile to the south of Melksham. It runs *via* HOLT JUNCTION and SEEND, to

DEVIZES (a telegraph station)

Is an ancient borough, in the centre of Wiltshire, with a population of 6,638. Its staple trade is woollen. St John's Church is somewhat remarkable, from the variety of architectural designs it displays. It returns two members to parliament.

Wilts, Somerset, etc, Main Line continued.

TROWBRIDGE

DISTANCE FROM STATION, ¼ MILE.
A TELEGRAPH STATION.
HOTEL – GEORGE.
MARKET DAY – SATURDAY.
FAIR – 5 AUGUST.

This town is the largest in the county, with the exception of Salisbury. It has a population of 9,626, and is situated on the river Ware. The church is large and highly decorated. It is one of the largest clothing towns in the west of England. Leland says of it, in his time even, 'it flourisheth by drapery.' Crabbe, the poet,

Bradford on Avon station
This is a fine Brunellian station. It was originally conceived by the Wilts, Somerset & Weymouth Railway, but delays in building the line meant it didn't open until 1857, by which time the line had become part of the GWR.

Left: An old photograph showing the tunnel and level crossing just to the east of the station itself. *(CMcC)*

Below: The station is a charming surviving example of Brunel's railway architecture. *(Bashereye)*

Left: Bradford on Avon's most iconic export is the bike with the little wheels. It was designed in 1962 by Alex Moulton, who also designed the rubber cone suspension system for the Mini car. The photograph shows the 1965 'New Look' Standard M1. The company was later sold to Raleigh, then bought back by Moulton in the early 1980s. The latest versions are described by the company as 'the original full-suspension, separable, small-wheeled, high-performance bicycle'. Prices range from £950 to over £16,000. *(G-Man)*

was rector here. George Keats, the poet, was a native. Ruins of *Farley Castle* (3 ½ miles) are very picturesque. A short branch here turns off to

BRADFORD (Branch)
A town that 'stondeth by clooth making,' said Leland, three centuries ago, and the same may be said of it now. The Avon is crossed by two bridges, one a very ancient one, with a chapel over one of the piers. This line continues its course, *via* FRESHFORD, LIMPLEY STOKE, and BATHAMPTON to
Bath (see page 18), a distance of 12 ½ miles from Trowbridge.

FROME
A telegraph station.
HOTELS – George, Crown.

Is agreeably situated on the north-east declivity of several hills contiguous to Selwood Forest. It has considerable manufactures of woollen cloth, and an excellent grammar school, founded by Edward VI. At *Nunney* (3 miles) are the ruins of a castle. *Marston Biggot* (2 miles) earl of Cork and Orrery. *Mells Park* (4 miles). *Longleat Park* (3 ½ miles) the extensive domain of the Marquis of Bath.
WITHAM JUNCTION, near which is *Witham Park*.

Wilts, Somerset etc, Main Line continued.

From Trowbridge we continue by the Valley of the Avon, with the grounds of *Rowed Ashton* and *Heywood House* on the left, and arrive at

WESTBURY
A telegraph station.
HOTEL – Lopez Arms.

This is an ancient borough, with a malting and broad cloth trade. Bryan Edwards, the historian, was a native. About two miles north-east is an ancient encampment, on the edge of the chalk downs near *Bratton*; on the escarpment below it is the figure of a white horse, the origin of which is doubtful and obscure. Four miles beyond is *Erle Stoke Park*, the seat of Lord Broughton.
We now bear to the left, leaving the Weymouth line on the

Salisbury Branch westbury To Salisbury

Our first station on this section of the Wilts, Somerset and Weymouth line, is that at

WARMINSTER
Telegraph station at Westbury, 4 ½ miles.
HOTELS – Bath Arms; Lamb.

Frome station

Situated on the former Wilts, Somerset & Weymouth Railway, this is a rare example of an all-over wooden roofed Brunellian station. There were others, such as nearby Bath, but they have all lost their roofs over the years. In truth the station was probably designed by one of his assistants, which was common practice.

Today the station is still used by Bristol to Weymouth trains, and some services to and from Bristol/Cardiff. The far platform is no longer accessible on foot and as can be seen from these photographs from 2005, the track and exposed platform area are becoming overgrown. The goods shed, visible in the distance in the upper picture, has been demolished.

This is a neat and respectable town, close to the western border of Salisbury Plain, on which, in the neighbourhood, are many remains of the old Britons. There is likewise a huge rampart and ditch called '*Old Ditch*' which may be attributed to the Saxons. The church is spacious and handsome. The tower is of the reign of Edward III.

Proceeding on our way with *Battlesbury*, *Middlesbury*, *Scratchbury*, *Cotley* and *Golden Barrow*, close by on our left (all ancient encampments), we arrive at

HEYTESBURY

TELEGRAPH STATION AT WESTBURY, 8 ½ MILES.

HOTELS – BATH ARMS; LAMB.

This town is situated in a pleasant valley on the river Wiley, with a population of 1,103, chiefly employed in the woollen manufacture. Here Queen Maude lived. In the ancient church (rebuilt in 1404) Cunningham, the antiquary, is buried. Close by is *Heytesbury House*, the seat of Lord Heytesbury. In the vicinity are more remains of our rude forefathers, in the shape of barrows, camps, entrenchments, and other earthworks, evidently occupied by Britons, Romans, Saxons, and Danes in succession. *Knock Castle*, 3 miles east, a more remarkable one than all.

Proceeding by the banks of the Wiley, we arrive at

CODFORD

TELEGRAPH STATION AT WESTBURY, 11 MILES.

In the vicinity are a Druidical circle on Codford Hill, *Bayton Hall*, A. B. Lambert, Esq.; *Bayton Church*, built in 1301, with an ancient font, and *Shockton House*. *Codford St Mary*'s Norman church is deserving a visit.

WILEY

TELEGRAPH STATION AT WILTON, 7 ¼ MILES.

In the neighbourhood are *Deptford Inn* (1/2 mile), *Fisherton de la Mere* (1 mile). *Yarmbury Castle* (2 miles), a most interesting earthen work or fortification, occupying an elevated situation above the plain. *Badbury Camp* (1 mile), supposed to be the *Mons Badonicus* of the Romans, and the *Baddiebrig* of the Saxons. Here Arthur defeated Cedric, in 520. The decayed town of *Hindon*, 6 miles west, near which is *Fonthill Abbey*, Alfred Morrison, Esq., but formerly the seat of Beckford, the author of that most original Eastern story, 'Caliph Vathek,' and has the appearance of a vast monastic edifice, crowned by a lofty tower, visible at the distance of 40 miles, and commands views over beautifully picturesque and abundantly diversified scenery. He died and was buried at Bath.

LANGFORD – In this vicinity are Steeple Langford, Hanging Langford,

Warminster and Salisbury

Above: Postcard view of the market place in Warminster, which has little changed. Apart from being a garrison town, Warminster is noted for the nearby lions at Longleat and also as a magnet for intergalactic visitors and associated UFO spotters.

Below: The train shed at Salisbury, photographed in 1938. Salisbury was served by the London & South Western Railway as well as the GWR, and station buildings remain from both. *(CMcC)*

Stapleford, Groveley Wood (here the Wiltshire hounds meet), and at East Castle, are earthworks 214 yards round. Groveley Castle contains 14 acres, is single ditched, with ramparts, and commands a beautiful view; and Hamshill, with its ditches: all of these are thought to have been British towns, occupied by the Romans. The train then proceeds on to

WISHFORD
TELEGRAPH STATION AT WILTON, 2 ½ MILES.

Here is an excellent Free Grammar School, and a handsome church. In the vicinity are South Newton and Wilton Woodford, at which the ancient Bishops of Sarum had a palace. Soon after we arrive at

WILTON
A TELEGRAPH STATION.
HOTEL – BELL, PEMBROKE ARMS.

WILTON is a place of great antiquity, and its importance is indicated by the circumstance of its having given name to the county. It was the scene of one of Alfred's victories over the Danes in 871; and the occasional residence of the West Saxon Kings. A Benedictine abbey, for nuns, existed here at an early period, of which Alfred and his successors, were great benefactors. The church was the abbey church. The new church is an elaborate imitation of the Lombard style, on which the Norman is founded. There is a county cross. It has much declined of late years: the population are partly engaged in the cloth and carpet factories. At that of Messrs Blackmore, the Axminster carpet, shewn at the Exhibition of 1851 from Gruner's designs, was manufactured. It is rather curious that this branch of manufacture was first introduced into England by a Frenchman of the name of Duffoly under the protection of the Herberts, in Elizabeth's time. Wilton Castle is built upon the site of the abbey; it was rebuilt by Wyatt. Here Sidney's sister, Pembroke's mother, lived, and Sir Philip wrote part of his *Arcadia*. The old castle was altered by Holbein and Inigo Jones, and visited by Charles I. here may be seen the old rusty arms of Sir William Herbert ap Thomas, which he wore when in France with Henry V. There is a fine collection of marbles, and portraits by Vandyke; Titian, by himself; Richard II, supposed to be the oldest oil painting extant; pictures by Rubens, etc. The park is beautifully timbered, having many very aged trees. John of Wilton, of the thirteenth century; John of Wilton, in the time of Edward III; Thomas of Wilton, in the time of Edward IV; and Massinger, the dramatist, were natives.

SALISBURY
DISTANCE FROM STATION, ¼ MILE. A TELEGRAPH STATION.
HOTELS – WHITE HART; RED LION; THREE SWANS.
OMNIBUSES AND COACHES TO STAPLEFORD, DEPTFORD, CRAFORD,

Salisbury

Above: The view looking across Salisbury, dominated by the Cathedral spire. *(LoC)*

Below left: A balloon winch vehicle at Larkhill on Salisbury Plain. In 1911 the No. 2 Air Battalion Royal Engineers was established at Larkhill and this was the first flying unit to use aeroplanes rather than balloons. However, activity and training with observation balloons did continue here. Note the fabric covered hangar in the background. *(CMcC)*

Below right: The stone circle at Stonehenge is only a mile away from Larkhill. These standing stones are now on the UNESCO list of World Heritage Sites, but in 1915 it was sold at auction along with 30 acres of land to a private owner for a princely £6,000. It is now owned by the Crown and managed by English Heritage, while the surrounding land is owned by the National Trust. *(LoC)*

HEYTESBURY, BOREHAM, SHAFTESBURY, WILTON, BARFORD, FOVANT, DONHEAD, LUDWELL, GILLINGHAM, MILBORNE PORT, SHERBORNE, WINCANTON, MERE, HINDON, KNOYLE, BODENHAM, CHARLTON, DOWNTON, BREAMORE, FORDINGBRIDGE, DEVIZES, BOSCOMB, PARK HOUSE, TIDWORTH, WOODYATES, THICKTHORN, BLANDFORD, WEYMOUTH, SHREWTON, LAVINGTON, WARDOUR, AND BOURNEMOUTH.

MARKET DAYS – TUESDAY AND SATURDAY; SECOND TUESDAY IN EVERY MONTH FOR CHEESE.

FAIRS – TUESDAYS AFTER 6 JANUARY, 25 MARCH, SECOND TUESDAY IN SEPTEMBER, SECOND TUESDAY AFTER 10 OCTOBER; FOR SHEEP, 15 JULY AND 30 OCTOBER.

Salisbury is a parliamentary borough (two members) and a bishop's see, in Wiltshire, at the terminus of a branch of the South Western line, 96 miles from London, on the rich green pastures of the Avon. Population 12,278. It is not an old town, compared with other sees, the real original Old Sarum being on the hill to the north of Salisbury, where the walls and ditches of the Roman *Sorbiodunum*, out of which it sprung, are easily traced, as well as roads branching from it. Here a Cathedral was planted after the Conquest (for which that of Sherborne was deserted), but in 1220 another migration took place, and the present magnificent edifice was begun by Bishop Poore. It was for the most part finished in the course of 32 years, so that it has the great advantage of being not only uniform in design but offers a complete specimen of the style of that age, namely, early English. The shape is a double cross, from end to end 442 feet long; through the greater transept the width is 203 feet, and 147 through the less. The west front (which with the spire is of later date than the body) is 130 feet wide and 200 high, and ornamented with niches, turrets, tracery, etc, and a large painted window; the lower eastern window is a very handsome new one, placed as a memorial to the late dean; the upper eastern window is a very splendid one – subject, the 'Brazen Serpent,' by Mortimer – the gift of a former Earl of Radnor. Above all rises a most beautiful *steeple*, consisting of a slender crocketted spire, 190 feet long, resting on a tower, which makes its total height from the ground above 400 feet. It is reported to be 22 inches out of the perpendicular; but whether or not it is a most imposing object from all points. There are said to be as many windows in the cathedral as days in the year. Several effigies and monuments are here – some as far back as the eleventh century, transferred of course from the old cathedral. Among them are a boy bishop, and William de Long epee (or Long-sword) son of Richard I, also Bishop Jewell, author of the *Apology for the English Church*, and Harris, the author of *Hermes*, and ancestor of the Malmesbury family. The last is a work of Bacon's; there are two by Flaxman. The cloisters are 190 feet square; they were restored by the late Bishop Denison. In the octagonal chapter house, besides the stained windows and carvings, there is a good library, the Salisbury Missal or Roman form of prayer, which was the model for all the rest, a carved table, etc, and an original copy of Magna Carta. At the large

Top: A fanciful print from around 1830 showing a Bristol & Exeter Railway train passing through Ashton vale with the Clifton Suspension bridge in the background. Brunel was engineer to both, but the bridge remained unfinished until after his death. The B&ER operated out of its own station at Temple Meads which was adjacent to the GWR terminus. *(CMcC)*

Right: This station at Flax Bourton, on the former B&ER Line to the south of Bristol, is post-Brunellian.

Below: As to be expected, Brunel built the B&ER line to his broad gauge. This massive locomotive from 1854 was designed by James Pearson and built in Bolton by Rothwell & Co.

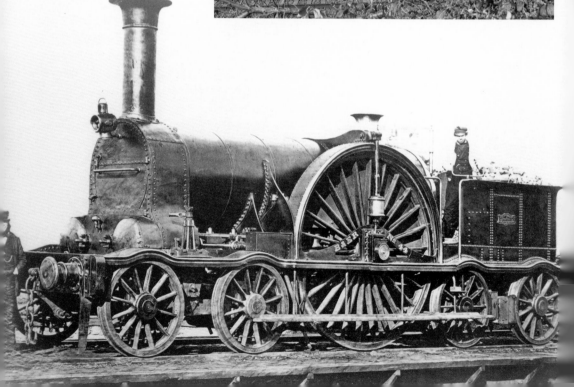

old palace is a series of portraits, beginning with Bishop Duppa of Charles I's time. Both the cathedral and city were fully examined by the members of the archaeological visit in 1844. Most of the streets, except the main one from Fisherton Street to Milford Hill, are laid out straight and regular, with rills 4 to 5 feet broad running through them from the Avon, Nadder and Wiley; but unfortunately the city lies low, and, though its water meadows are pleasant to look at, the courts in which the poor live are in a filthy state. The *Council Chamber* was built 1795 by Sir R. Taylor; portraits of James I, Queen Anne, etc. St Thomas' church is Gothic; it contains a carved monument of wood. Large county gaol at Fisherton, built 1822. St Edmund's Church, at the north-east corner of the city, was once collegiate. South of Milford Hill is St Martin's, and in the centre of the city stands St Thomas'. The churches are all about the same age. From the close behind the palace, an ancient bridge of the thirteenth century crosses the Avon to Harnham. There are two grammar schools; in that belonging to the city *Addison* was educated, at the Cathedral Grammar School in the close. He was born at Millston, higher up the river. There are also several hospitals and charities; one being a college for the widows of clergymen, founded by Bishop Seth Ward – another, a set of alms-houses by Bishop Poore – and a third, a hospital by Longsword's wife, Ella.

WESTON-SUPER-MARE BRANCH

Bristol and Exeter Main Line

After leaving Yatton we catch a very pleasing view of the Channel, with its dimpled surface spotted with white sails, and its range of ruddy headlands stretching far away in the distance. Green hills, diversified by open downs and richly cultivated corn lands, constitute a delightful contrast in the opposite direction; and thus, amid a varied succession of prospects, we reach the station at

BANWELL
DISTANCE FROM STATION, 2¼ MILES.
TELEGRAPH STATION AT YATTON, 3½ MILES.

This little village has become of some notoriety from the discovery of two caverns in its vicinity, one called the Stalactite, and the other the Bone Cave, which attract a great number of visitors. Locking and Hatton adjacent, with their antiquated churches – the cavern of Woke, and the Chees – celebrated cliffs of Cheddar, are all worth visiting.

Leaving the Banwell station, we pass the villages of Wick, St Lawrence, Kewstoke, and further on, Worle Hill, which commands a series of extensive maritime and inland views, and variegated landscapes.

WESTON-SUPER-MARE Junction.

Weston-super-Mare

At the start of the nineteenth century Weston-super-Mare was a little fishing community. The Victorian fashion for seaside holidays, in no small part prompted by Bradshaw's publications, saw it grow very rapidly into one of the busiest holiday resorts in the south-west.

Top: Birnbeck Pier opened in 1867 and it is sometimes referred to as the 'old pier' to differentiate it from Weston's main pier. The Birnbeck Pier is the only one in the mainland to link with an island.
Left and below: More views of Weston including The Parade from Anchor Road, and a bandstand in the park. *(LoC)*

WESTON-SUPER-MARE – (Branch)

DISTANCE FROM STATION, 2 MILES.
A TELEGRAPH STATION.
HOTEL – BATH.

WESTON-SUPER-MARE has the advantage of being very accessible from Bristol, Bath, Exeter, and other towns on the line of the Great Western Railway. It has none of the picturesqueness arising from old streets and buildings, but, situated on the margin of Uphill Bay, near the Bristol Channel, it possesses the usual attractions of a neat watering place, having within the last ten years become considerably enlarged and frequented. The receding of the tide leaves a disfiguring bank of mud along the beach, which is a great drawback to the enjoyment of bathing; but a good market, numerous shops, and a delightful neighbourhood for rambling, present some counterbalancing advantages.

Worle Hill is one of the pleasantest spots that a tourist could desire to meet with. In traversing the northern or sea side of the hill, the path lies, most of the way, through a copse of young fir trees, presenting occasional openings of the Channel and the rocky coast beyond. Towards the eastern end of the hill beautiful prospects are unfolded over a large and richly cultivated plain, extending to Woodspring Prior and Clevedon, with two or three churches standing up amid the elms and ashes. The nearest of these is Kewstone Church, situated on the slop of Worle Hill itself. It derives its name from St Kew, who once formed his cell on the bleak hill top. From the church a craggy track, called the Pass of St Kew, consisting of a hundred natural and artificial steps, leads over the hill to the village of Milton on the opposite side, and these are said to have been worn by the feet of the pious recluse, as he daily went to perform his devotions at the church, which then occupied the same spot as it does at present. The ruins of the Priory at Woodspring are of considerable extent, and very picturesque, situated in a very solitary position at the farther end of a wide marshy but cultivated flat; they are divided form the sea by a narrow ridge of rocks, called Swallow Cliffs, quite out of the way of any frequented road. Crossing the broad mossy top of Worle Hill we can descend upon the village or slope of the hill, and commands a delightful view over the richly cultivated flat to the range of the Mendip Hills.

In short, the inducements to prolong a visit to Weston will be found principally to arise from the charming localities by which it is surrounded. The climate is bracing, and the air is very salubrious.

Left: The change of gauge at Grange Court in August 1869.

Below: This stone abutment at New Passage marks the site of the pier for Brunel's Bristol & South Wales Union Railway. Before the coming of the Severn Tunnel and bridges, passengers travelled by train to the pier and took a ferry across to Portskewett, where they continued by train to South Wales.

Swansea Docks
Right: On 29 November 1865 a train of the Vale of Neath Railway plunged from a bridge at Swansea's North Dock, killing both driver and stoker. Swansea Docks is the collective name for several docks located to the east of the city centre.

Branches in South Wales

Gloucester to Newport

This line of railway affords great facilities to tourists and lovers of the picturesque for visiting the beautiful scenery of Wales.

Gloucester is now the central point of communication between the north and the south, the east and the west of the kingdom. From Plymouth there is an uninterrupted run though Bristol and Gloucester into the farthest points of the north where the iron road has yet pierced its way.

Upon starting, the line proceeds over an embankment and viaduct over the low meadows near the Severn, and then passes over the two bridges, and continues along the west bank of the Severn. The beautiful spire of Highnam new church appears in view, and is quickly left behind, and in a few minutes the train reaches the first station on the line, which is called 'Oakle Street,' a rural spot, convenient for Churcham.

Grange Court Juction – Westbury-upon-Severn, 1 mile distant. The trains of the Hereford, Ross, and Gloucester Railway turn off at this station to the right.

[Gloucester to Hereford branch line – see page 59]

We here leave the county of Gloucester, and enter that of

MONMOUTHSHIRE

A small English county, bordering on the principality of Wales, which, in point of fertility, picturesque scenery, and historic remains, is the most interesting district, in proportion to its size, of any in the kingdom. The general aspect of this county is inviting, both from its diversity and fertility. A continual recurrence of hill and dale, wood and water, corn fields and meadows; the sublimity of wildly magnificent, and the beauty of mild and cultivated, scenery, combine to delight the eye of the beholder at every turn he takes in this district. Nor is the air less congenial to health than the face of the country is interesting to view. The river Wye, which runs through this county, is celebrated for its picturesque scenery. The peculiar characteristic of this beautiful river are its sinuous course, the uniformity of its breadth, and the variegated scenery on its banks. So considerable is its serpentine course, that the distance from Ross to Chepstow, which is not seventeen miles in a direct line, is by water forty-three. The effects of this sinuosity are numerous, diversified, and striking; and they principally arise from two circumstances,

Left: Opening of the Swansea & Neath Railway with the first train passing Neath Abbey station.
Below: Scene of the 1911 accident near Pontypridd, in which eleven people were killed. Pontypridd is said to have had the longest station platform in the world, and the lower image shows fodder being collected for the pit ponies during the 1910 coal strike. *(CMcC)*

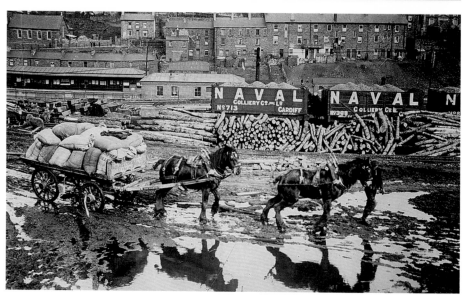

the mazy course of the river, and the loftiness of its banks. In consequence of this, the views is exhibits are of the most beautiful kind of perspective. From the constant shifting of the foreground and side screens, the same objects are seen from a variety of sides, and in different points of view.

[Newport to Monmouthshire line – see below]

NEATH
POPULATION, 6,810.
A TELEGRAPH STATION.
HOTEL – CASTLE.
MARKET DAY – WEDNESDAY.
FAIRS – LAST WEDNESDAY IN MARCH, TRINITY THURSDAY, JULY 31ST, SEPTEMBER 12TH, AND LAST WEDNESDAY IN OCTOBER.

Neath is a coal and mining port, with an ancient castle, and some abbey ruins. Here the fine Vale of Neath may be ascended to the beautiful waterfalls at its summit *(see Merthyr Tydvil, page 91).*

VALE OF NEATH RAILWAY

Neath to Merthyr
From Neath we again turn out of our course, and pass the stations of Aberdylais, Resolven, and Glyn Neath. From this point, *Craig-y-linn*, the highest mountain in Glamorganshire, with its lakes and ravines, and which here makes a bold horse-shoe sweep, raising its huge bulk against the sky, may be reached.

HIRWAIN, junction of line to Aberdare, LLYDCOED, and ABERNANT stations follow, arriving at

MERTHYR TYDVIL.

[Branch line from Newport]

MONMOUTHSHIRE LINE
The Eastern and Western Valleys Lines turn off at this point to the right, passing through districts rich in mineral products, but not of essential importance to the general tourist. The stations on the Western Line are BASSALLEG JUNCTION, TYDEE, RISCA, CROSS KEYS, CHAPEL BRIDGE, ABERCARNE, NEW BRIDGE, CRUMLIN, LLANHILLETH, ABERBEEG, CWM, VICTORIA, EBBW VALE, ABERTILLERY, and BLAINA. Those on the eastern Branch, LLANTANAM, CWMBRAN, PONTNEWYDD, PONTRHYDYRUN, PONTPOOL, PONTNEWYNNYDD, ABERSYCHAN, CWM AVON, and BLAENAVON.

Returning to Newport we now proceed by the
WEST MIDLAND

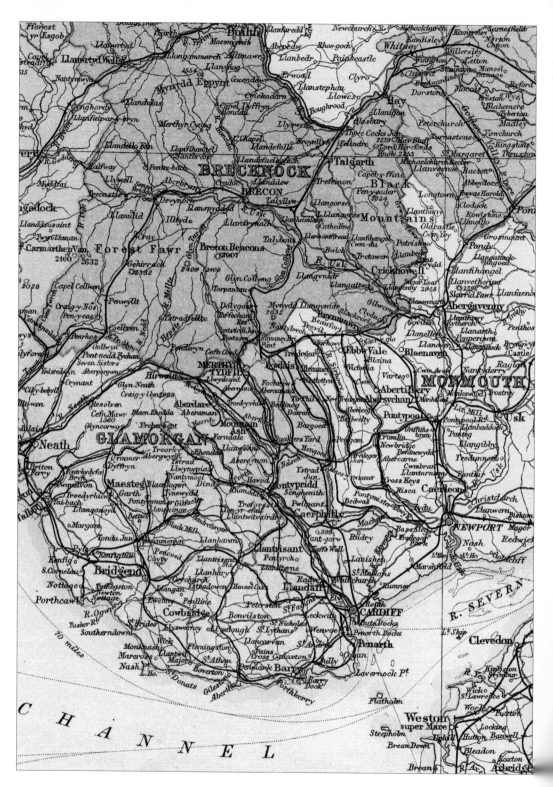

Map from *Bartholmew's Gazeteer*, 1932. *(CMcC)*

Newport to Abergavenny and Hereford.

In ten minutes after leaving Newport we reach PONTTNEWYDD, and in ten minutes more, the station

PONTYPOOL ROAD.

DISTANCE FROM THE TOWN OF THE SAME NAME, 1 MILE.
A TELEGRAPH STATION.

Near is *Pontypool Park*, Hanbury Leigh Esq. This forms the junction with the

TAFF VALE EXTENSION.

A short line, 16 miles long, running into the Taff vale Line at Quaker's Yard. The stations on the line are PONTYPOOL, CRUMLIN, TREDEGAR, RHYMNEY JUNCTION, LLANCAICH, and QUAKER'S YARD.

Merthyr Tydvil, see page 91.

COLEFORD, MONMOUTH, USK, AND PONTYPOOL.

Pontypool Road to Monmouth.

About a mile and a half beyond Pontypool Road this line turns off; and at the distance of about 3½ miles further, we cross the river at Usk, and stop at the station of that name.

USK.

The town is situated a little to the right of the station, and is a place of great antiquity. Considerable remains of a castle where Richard III and Edward IV are reputed to have been born, are to be seen; likewise part of a priory. Fine salmon fishing.

Llangibby Castle (3 miles).

Passing LLANDENNY Station, we arrive at

RAGLAN ROAD,

Which is available for foot passengers only.

Here are the fine remains of the castle built by Sir W. Thomas in the 14th century. The Marquis of Worcester defended it for four years against the Parliament: it is now a most picturesque ruin. It gives title of Baron Raglan to a descendant – the late Lord Fitzroy Somerset, Commander-in-Chief in the late war in the Crimea. He was military secretary to Wellington, and lost an arm at Waterloo. What it was in the 16th century we may hear from the poet Churchyard; he speaks of it as –

A CASTLE FINE THAT RAGLAN HIGHT – STANDS MOTED ALMOST ROUND,
MADE OF FREESTONE, UPRIGHT, STRAIGHT AS LINE,
WHOSE WORKMANSHIP IN BEAUTY DOTH ABOUND.

Monmouth

Left: Two bridges over the River Minnow at Monmouth. A print dated 1799 showing the old Tibbs footbridge with St Mary's Church in the background. And the fortified gateway of the Minnow Bridge from around 1890. *(LoC)*

Left This statue to the pioneer motorist and aviator Charles Rolls stands in front of the Shire Hall in Agincourt Square, Monmouth. Rolls died during a flying display held at Bournemouth in 1910. His family were significant landowners in the Monmouth area and they had the statue erected in his memory.

DINGESTOW

Or Dynstow. In a barn, among beautiful orchards, may be seen the remains of Grace Dieu Abbey.

MONMOUTH.

TELEGRAPH STATION AT PONTYPOOL ROAD, 18 MILES.
HOTELS – BEAUFORT ARMS; KING'S HEAD.

MONMOUTH, the capital of Monmouthshire, is on a delightful part of the Wye, at the junction of the Monnow, a parliamentary borough, returning one member, conjointly with Newport and Usk, with an agricultural population of 5,710, which is rather on the decrease; but this will no doubt be augmented by the recent opening of the railway from Pontypool. It was the ancient *Blestium*, from which a Roman road, in the direction of the present one, went to Usk. There was a castle here, even in Saxon times, which afterwards became the residence of Henry IV, and here, in 1387, his famous son Henry V was born – 'Harry of Monmouth' – the immortal Prince Hal of Shakespeare.

The few remains of this castle (which belongs to the Duke of Beaufort), stand among houses on a ridge over the Monnow, to the west near the gaol, the walls being 6 to 10 feet thick. Here is shown the room in which Henry was born, and the great hall by the side of it. There is a statue of him in the Market Place.

Within a short distance of the town are the following objects of notice: The *Wye*, so celebrated for its uniform breadth, lofty cliffs, winding course, and picturesque scenery, which is perpetually changing its character. Elegant and commodious boats are kept here for the use of tourists. 'The stranger cannot do better than hire Samuel Dew, whom he will find by Monmouth Bridge. Sam is one of the steadiest and cleverest of Wye watermen, knows the river well, and is quite used to guiding those who are in search of the beautiful.' – *The Land we Live in.*

Near the junction of the Trothey, about a mile from Monmouth, is *Troy House*, an old seat of the Duke of Beaufort, with old portraits and gardens, where the marquis of Worcester gave Charles I a dish of fruit 'from Troy.' 'Truly my lord,' said the king, 'I have heard that corn grows where Troy stood, but I never thought that there had grown apricots there before.' Here is Henry's cradle (so called), and the armour he wore at Agincourt. About 6 miles down the Wye is Beacon Hill, 1,000 feet high, near Trelech Cross (three Druid stones), and below that Landogo Bigswear, Tintern Abbey, Wyndcliffe, Chepstow (17 miles by water); *Wonastow*, seat of Sir W. Pilkington, baronet, is a very old seat, which belonged to the Herberts. *Treowen*, near it, is another, but now turned into a farm house. Up the Trothey is *Llantillio House.*

A pretty road leads to Beaulieu Grove on the top, near the handsome spire church of Lantillio Crossenny, and the ruins of White Castle, a fortress built by the early Norman possessors of this county. In ascending the beautiful

83

Workman (politely, to old lady, who has accidentally got into a smoking compartment). "You don't object to my pipe, I 'ope, mum?"
Old Lady. "Yes, I do object, very strongly!"
Workman. "Oh! Then out you get!!"

Punch on the railways
Three Victorian cartoons from *Mr Punch's Railway Book.*

Impatient Traveller. "Er—how long will the next train be, portah?"
Porter. "Heaw long? Weel, sir ah dunno heaw ah con saay to hauf an inch. Happen there'll be fower or five co-aches an' a engine or soa."

Punch's style of humour might not have the modern reader rolling in the aisles, but it does offer an insight into the nuances of nineteenth-century railway travel. As these examples show, the interaction between the townies and country folk was a frequent source of hilarity.

NOT QUITE UP TO DATE

Somerset Rustic (on seeing the signal drop). "Ar don't know if it'd make any difference, maister, but thic ther' bit o' board of yourn 'ave a fallen down!"

valley of the Monnow, there are two other castles worth notice – Skenfrith and Grosmont – the latter being under Greig Hill, near a small cross church. Most of these structures were formerly part of the Duchy of Lancaster, through John of Gaunt, but now belong, with large possessions, to the Beaufort family. From Monmouth, up the Wye, you pass Dixton Church, a pretty rustic building; then New Weir, Symond's Yat, Courtfield (where Henry V was nursed), &c, till you come to Ross. But the best plan is to descend from that place (see the *Wye*).

An excursion may be made to the *Forest of Dean*, and its interesting scenery. You pass (taking the Coleford Road) the Buckstone, an immense Logan stone, on a hill, 56 feet round at the top, and tapering off to 3 at the bottom. Coleford Church is modern, the old one having been destroyed in the civil wars, when Lord Herbert routed some of the parliament people here. About 3 miles north-east is the Speech House, where the miners hold their meetings. To the south, in the direction of Offa's Dyke, which may still be traced, is *Clearwell Park*, the seat of the dowager Countess of Dunraven, where a great heap of Roman money was found in 1847, and St. Briaval's, with its *May Pole* and hundred court, part of a Norman castle. There are many deserted mines. The wood is cut for hoops, poles, and other purposes.

A good stone bridge across the Wye, and one the Monnow – an ancient stone building, called the Welsh Gate, with a Norman chapel (St. Thomas's) at the foot. Many of the houses are white-washed, and, as they are dispersed among gardens and orchards, the view of the town in summer is picturesque. The parish church of *St. Mary* has a tapering spire 200 feet. It was attached to a priory, of which there are remains in a private house adjoining. The handsome oriel window is called the 'study' of Geoffrey of Monmouth, but he was born in the 11th century, long before such a style was invented. He was a Welsh monk (Geoffrey ap Arthur), who turned the British Chronicles, fables and all, into rugged Latin. To him, however, we are indebted for Shalespeare's King Lear, and the Sabrina of Milton's *Comus*.

Monmouth was once famous for its woollen caps, 'the most ancient, general, warm, and profitable covering for men's heads on this island,' according to Fuller. The manufacture was afterwards transferred to Bewdley. This is, or was, a capper's chapel in the church, 'better carved and gilded than any other part of it.' Fletcher takes care to remember this.

The well-endowed free school was founded by W. Jones, who, from a poor shop-boy at this place, became a rich London merchant. Newland was his birth-place; and there, after quitting London, he showed himself under the disguise of poverty, but being told to try for relief at Monmouth, where he had been at service, he repaired hither, was kindly received, and then revealed who he was.

One of the walks is at Chippenham meadow, near the junction of the Monnow and Wye, under a grove of elms. Anchor and May Hills are good points of view. Past May Hill (across the Wye) is *Kymin Hill*, the east half of which is Gloucestershire.

Abergavenny
Above: Abergavenny and the Holy Mountain, Photocrom image *c.* 1890. *(LoC)*
Below: A 1960s postcard showing a remarkably quiet Frogmore Street in Abergavenny. *(CMcC)*

Pontypool Road to Abergavenny

Passing the station of NANTYDERRY, or Goitre, we arrive at PENPERGWM, near which is Llanover, the seat of Lord Llanover, and three miles to the right is Clytha. Proceeding along the valley of the USk, we soon arrive at,

ABERGAVENNY.
  A telegraph station.
  HOTEL – Angel.
  MARKET DAY – Tuesday.
  FAIRS – Third Tuesday in March, May 14th, June 24th (wool), Tuesday before July 20th, September 25th, and November 19th.
  RACES in April.

This interesting old place, of 4,621 inhabitants, stands among the Monmouthshire Hills, near the Sugar Loaf, Blorenge, and other peaks, in a fine part of Usk, where the Gavenny joins it, and gives name to the town, which the Romans who had a station here, called *Gobannium*. It was formerly noted for its old castle and springs, founded by Hammeline de Balun at the Conquest, the former for the purpose of guarding the pass into Wales. This feudal structure afterwards came to the Nevilles, who still take title from it. A Tudor gate, from which there is a fine prospect, is the chief remain. Later still Abergavenny became celebrated for its Welsh wigs, made of goats' hair, some of which sold at 40 guineas each. Physicians also used to send patients here to drink goats' whey. But its present prosperity arises from its flannel weaving, and the valuable coal and iron works at Clydach, Blaenavon, &c., in the neighbourhood – a state of things likely to be much increased by the Newport, Abergavenny and Hereford Railway, part of the important chain which unites South Wales to Liverpool and the north of England.

The old bridge of 15 arches crosses the Usk. The church has some ancient tombs of the Beauchamps, and other possessors of the lordship. Traces of the old priory exist near it. There is also an old grammer school, and a modern Cymreidiggion Society's Hall for Welsh bardic meetings – Monmouth being essentially Welsh, though separated from the principality since Henry VIII's time. Antiquaries say that until feudal tenures were abolished by Charles II, Abergavenny castle used to give its holders their title by mere possession – like Arundel Castle, in Sussex, instead of by writ or by patent.

The views from the Sugar Loaf, which is 1,856 feet high, are magnificent. It takes three hours to ascend it. A still more beautiful prospect is enjoyed from St. Michael's old Chapel on Skyrrid Vawr. The White Castle is near the mountain. Raglan Castle, which the famous marquis of Worcester held out so stoutly against Cromwell, is also near (8 miles), on the Monmouth Road. Its machicolated gate, hall, chapel, the yellow tower, &c., are in excellent

Industrial valleys

Left: An early view of a mine in the Rhondda Valley. The railways provided a vital link between the valleys and the docks at Cardiff, Newport and Swansea.

Middle and lower: Bradshaw writes about the Dowlais Ironworks and Steelworks. 'Visitors should see the furnaces by night when the red glare of the flames produces an uncommonly striking effect.' Founded in 1759, from the mid-nineteenth century it was run by Lady Charlotte Guest and Edward Divett following the death of Edward Guest. The pair revived the company through the adoption of the Bessemer process for steel production. Lady Guest died in 1895. Her daughter-in-law's name is commemorated in the name of works loco No. 33, *Lady Cordelia.* The main works survived until the 1930s, with production ceasing at Dowlais in 1936. *(CMcC)*

preservation, through the care of its owner, the Duke of Beaufort. Llanthony Abbey stands in a wild part of the Hhondu. The scenery of the Usk, from Abergavenny up to Brecon, is very romantic, as it winds round the black mountains, in one of the highest peaks of which it rises above Trecastle. Excellent trout fishing.

The Merthyr Tredegar, and Abergavenny Railway runs out to the left at this place, and will, when finished, prove to be a very valuable link in the railway system, as there will be direct communication between the more westerly districts of South Wales and those of the Midland Counties. That part of the line open at present passes through GOVILAN and GILWERNB to BRYNMAWR. The rest of the journey through Tredegar to Merthyr is performed by coach, which runs once a day each way, in connection with one of the trains.

LLANFIHANGEL and PANDY stations.

PONTRILAS.
TELEGRAPH STATION AT HEREFORD, 10¾ MILES.
MONEY ORDER OFFICE AT HEREFORD.

ST. DEVERAUX and TRAM INN stations being passed, we shortly arrive at Hereford, particulars of which will be found on page 59.

[Branch from Cardiff on the Taff Vale to Merthyr and Brecon]

TAFF VALE

Cardiff to Aberdare and Merthyr.

LLANDAFF.
POPULATION, 6,585.
TELEGRAPH STATION AT CARDIFF, 3½ MILES.
HOTEL – RAILWAY.
MONEY ORDER OFFICE AT CARDIFF.

LLANDAFF, a small decayed village, but the seat of a diocese, founded in the 5th century, having a half ruined *Cathedral*, 270 feet long, chiefly in the early English style. The south door is Norman. Some old monuments are seen – one being ascribed to Dubritias, the first bishop.

From Llandaff, in the course of about half an hour, we are hurried past the stations of WALNUT TREE Junction, TREFOREST, and NEWBRIDGE, the junction of the Rhondda Valley line, via PORTH to YSTRAD and TREHERBERT.

Above left: The image of Welsh national costume was popularised in the nineteenth century through the spread of railway travel, tourism and the development of photography. *(LoC)*
Above right: The faces of the miners at a Monmouth colliery. The coalfields of South Wales fueled Britain's industrial might and they continued in production well into the twentieth century. *(CMcC) Below:* A South Wales colliery village, Llwnypia in the Rhondda Fawr Valley. Note the close proximity of the houses and the working mine. *(LoC)*

ABERDARE BRANCH.

MOUNTAIN ASH and TREAMAN stations.

ABERDARE.
POPULATION, 32,299.
A telegraph station.
HOTELS – Boot and railway.
MARKET DAY – Saturday.
FAIRS – April 1st and 16th, November 13th.

The scenery of the vale of Cynon here is charming. A little beyond there is a junction with the Vale of Neath Railway to Merthyr (see page 79).

Taff Vale Main Line continued.
QUAKER'S YARD and TROEDYRHIEW stations.

MERTHYR.
POPULATION, 83,875.
A telegraph station.
HOTELS – Castle, Bush.
MARKET DAYS – Wednesday and Saturday.
BANKERS – Wilkins and Co.; Branch of West of England and South Wales District Banking Company.

MERTHYR TYDVIL is a parliamentary borough, the great mining town, in South Wales, 21 miles from Cardiff, with which there is a railway communication by a branch out of the South Wales line. It stands up the Taff, among the rugged and barren-looking hills in the north-east corner of Glamorganshire, the richest county in Wales for mineral wealth. About a century ago the first iron works were established here, since which the extension has been amazingly rapid. Blast furnaces, forges, and rolling mills are scattered on all sides. Each iron furnace is about 55 feet high, containing 5,000 cubic feet; and capable of smelting 100 tons of pig-iron weekly, as there are upwards of 50, the annual quantity of metal may be tolerably estimated; but great as the supply may seem, it is scarcely equal to the demand created for it by railways. The largest works are those belonging to Lady Guest and Messers. Crawshay, where 3,000 to 5,000 hands are employed. At Guest's Dowlais works there are 18 or 20 blast furnaces, besides many furnaces for puddling, balling, and refining; and 1,000 tons of coal a day are consumed.

Visitors should see the furnaces by night when the red glare of the flames produces an uncommonly striking effect. Indeed, the town is best visited at that time, for by day it will be found dirty, and irregularly built, without order or management, decent roads or footpaths, no supply of water, and no public building of the least note, except Barracks, and a vast Poor-House, lately finished, in the shape of a cross, on heaps of the rubbish accumulated

Brecon
Left: The town centre.
(Velela)
Below: View across the town to the beautiful Brecon Hills.
(Immanuel Giel)

Above: Double locomotive *Mountaineer,* built in 1866. Operated for a short time on the Anglesey Central Railway, it was also used on the Neath & Brecon Railway for a time.

from the pits and works. Cholera and fever are, of course, at home here, in scenes which would shock even the most 'eminent defender of the filth,' and which imperatively demand that their Lady owner should become one of 'the Nightingale sisterhood' for brief space of time. Out of 695 couples married in 1845, 1,016 persons signed with marks, one great secret of which social drawback is the unexampled rapidity with which the town has sprung up; but we hope that proper measures will be taken henceforth by those who draw enormous wealth from working these works, to improve the condition of the people. Coal and iron are found together in this part of wales, the coal being worked mostly by levels, in beds 2 to 3 feet thick. Besides the large and small works in and about Merthyr, there are those at Aberdare (a growing rival to Merthyr), Herwain, Pentwain, Blaenavon, Brynmawr, Nantyglo, Ebbew (w as oo) Vale, Beaufort, Tredegar, Rhimney, Sirhowy, &c., nearly all seated at the head of the valleys, and many of them being in the neighbouring county of Monmouth, which, though reckoned part of England, is essentially Welsh in its minerals, scenery, and people. Railways and canals now traverse these valleys to the sea.

Merthyr Tydvil, as well as its church, derives its name, signifying the Martyr Tydvil, from St. Tudfyl, the daughter of Brysham (a Welsh chief) who was put to death for her religion in the early ages of the British church. Many such confessors are commemorated in the designation bestowed on parishes in Wales.

In the neighbourhood are the following objects of notice. The Taff may be ascended to Quaker's Yard and Newbridge, where there are large metal works, and a bridge, called Pont-y-Prid in Welsh, remarkable as the production of a self-taught local architect, named Edwards, who built it in 1751. It is a single arch, with a rise of one-fourth of the span, which is 140 feet, yet it is only 2½feet thick in the crown. Once and twice it fell when completed, but the third time the builder was successful, experience having taught him to diminish the strain from its own weight, by boring three large holes on each side near the piers. Following the Neath rail, you come to Pont-neath-Vaughan, at the head of the fine Vale of Neath, within a few miles of which are the Hefeste, Purthin, and its branches, which are 40 to 70 or 80 feet down. One on the Mellte is particularly worth notice, as it flows for half-a-mile through a limestone cave, and then re-appears just before it sweeps down a fall of 40 feet, with so clean a curve that people have actually taken shelter from the rain under it, on a narrow ledge in the face of the rock. The smaller spouts are called Sewbs (w as oo). These are all in Brecknockshire; but there is one of 90 feet at Merlin Court, half-way down the Vale of Neath; and to the right of this an ancient Roman way, called Sarn Helen, or via Julia Montana, may yet be traced. It went from an important Roman station. The direct road from Merthyr to Brecon is through a lofty pass, called Glyn Tarrell, having the Brecnockshire Beacons, 2,862 feet high on one side, and Mount Cafellente, 2,394 feet high, on the other. A considerable portion of this route has been laid with rails, and with the exception of a small portion from Merthyr to Dowlais, which is at present performed by coach, is in operation.

The route lies through DOWLAIS, DOLYGAER, TALYBONT, and TALLYLLYN to

BRECON.

TELEGRAPH STATION AT ABERGAVENNY, 21 MILES.

HOTELS – THE CASTLE; SWAN.

MARKET DAYS – WEDNESDAYS AND SATURDAYS.

FAIRS – FIRST WEDNESDAY IN MARCH, JULY 5, SEPTEMBER 9, NOVEMBER 16; ALSO IN MARCH AND NOVEMBER 16, FOR HIRING.

RACES IN SEPTEMBER.

This place is situated in the midst of very beautiful mountain scenery, has a population of 5,673, returning one member to parliament. It is 20 miles from Abergavenny, and communicable by coach every day. The principle buildings consist of three churches, County Hall, and Market House, very handsome new Assize Courts, built in 1843, Barracks, Theatre, Infirmary, a bridge of seven arches over the USK, from which is a fine view; there are also an Independent Training College and Grammar School at which Jones, the county historian, was educated.

Here are the remains of an old castle, consisting of the 'Ely Tower', so called from Dr. Morton, Bishop of Ely, who was a prisoner at the instance of Richard III, and as the scene of the conference between the Bishop and the Duke of Buckingham. Newmarch, a Norman baron, was the founder of the castle. Hugh Price, the founder of Jesus College, at Oxford, was born here; and Shakespeare's Fluellen, or Sir David Gow lived in the neighbourhood. He was knighted at Agincourt by Henry V, when at the point of death, having sacrificed his own life to save the king's. Another native of the Brecon was Mrs. Siddons. The 'Shoulder of Mutton' Inn is pointed out as the place of her nativity. It stands in a romantic part of the Usk, by the banks of which beautiful walks are laid out. To the north of it (22 miles by the lower and 17 by the upper road) is Builth. There are good sulphur springs in this quarter, viz: Park Wells, Llanwrtyd Wells, Llandrindod Wells, &c. Making the descent of the Usk you come to Crickhowell, where there is good angling, and (what is rare in the county) a spire church.

A postscript:

The Battle of Mickleton Tunnel

One event not mentioned by Bradshaw was the last battle between private armies held on British soil, and naturally Brunel was in the thick of it. The Mickleton Hill is just to the north-west of Chipping Camden on the Oxford, Worcester & Wolverhampton Railway's line heading towards Honeybourne and Evesham. By the summer of 1851 progress on the tunnel and the long approach cuttings was going far too slowly for IKB's liking and when a dispute arose with the contractors regarding the contract and payments he resolved to occupy the works. Some accounts say that Brunel's army of navvies was 2,000 strong. Magistrates and the police were called and the Riot Act was read before the matter was resolved.

Top: The entrance to Mickleton Tunnel. *(Network Rail) Left:* Navvies are the unsung heroes of the railways. J. C. Bourne's depiction of navvies at work on the GWR, and their twentieth-century equivalent. *(CMcC)*

Michael Portillo with the author, John Christopher, at Paddington station in 2012 during filming for the *Great British Railway Journeys* television series.

More Bradshaw's Guides from Amberley

Acknowledgements

I would like to acknowledge and thank the many individuals and organisations who have contributed to the production of this book. Unless otherwise stated all new photography is by the author. Additional images have come from a number of sources and I am grateful to the following: The US Library of Congress *(LoC)*, Campbell McCutcheon *(CMcC)*, The US National Archives & Records Administration *(NARA)*, Network Rail, The Nationaal Archief, Netherlands, Ibagli, Hugh Llewelyn, Mertbiol, Stanley C. Jenkins, Tejvan Pettinger, Juhertum, Velela, Immanuel Giel, David Hunt, G-Man, Andrew Helme, Arpingstone and Bashereye. Apologies to anyone left out unknowingly and any such errors brought to my attention will be corrected in subsequent editions. Thanks also to Eleri Pipien at Amberley for additional picture research. *JC*